SUICIDE... DON'T DO IT

Jackie Calloway

Largo, MD

© 2021 Jackie Calloway

All rights reserved under the international copyright law. No part of this book may be reproduced or transmitted in any form or by any means, electronic or mechanical, including photocopying, recording, or by any information storage and retrieval system, without the express, written permission of the publisher or the author. The exception is reviewers, who may quote brief passages in a review.

Christian Living Books, Inc.
P.O. Box 7584
Largo, MD 20792
christianlivingbooks.com
We bring your dreams to fruition.

ISBN 9781562295295

Unless otherwise indicated, all Scripture quotations are from the King James Version of the Bible. Scripture quotations marked NKJV are taken from The New King James Version / Thomas Nelson Publishers, Nashville: Thomas Nelson Publishers, Copyright © 1982. Used by permission. All rights reserved. Scripture quotations marked AMP are taken from the Amplified Bible, Copyright © 1954, 1958, 1962, 1964, 1965, 1987 by The Lockman Foundation. Used by permission.

Contents

Dedication v

Chapter 1. I Don't Want to Live Anymore 1

Chapter 2. Fear Was the Darkroom Where Satan
Developed My Negatives 7

Chapter 3. What Was I Thinking? 11

Chapter 4. Save the Children 23

Chapter 5. What Would Daddy Say? 27

Chapter 6. What About Tim? 31

Chapter 7. Stop the Wedding! 35

Chapter 8. Pregnancy And The Great Pretender 39

Chapter 9. Soul Ties and Suffering 45

Chapter 10. I Waited Patiently for the Lord 51

Chapter 11. God Knows My Name! 55

Chapter 12. Encourage Yourself Jackie Smith 61

Chapter 13. It's a Beautiful Girl 65

Chapter 14. The After Shock! 69

Chapter 15. More Difficult Days Ahead 73

Chapter 16. A New Life in View 79

Chapter 17. It Won't Be as Long as It's Been Bein' 83

Chapter 18. Love on the Horizon 87

Chapter 19. Trust God All the Way 97

Chapter 20. God Does All Things Well 99

Chapter 21. Another Turn of Events 103

Chapter 22. Who Is Margo Really? 107

Chapter 23. The Conclusion of the Matter 111

Acknowledgments *119*

About the Author *121*

Dedication

I DEDICATE THIS BOOK TO all of my children and grandchildren who were spared, by the grace of God, after my suicide attempt. Margo, Rhonda, Chaunci, Elyse, Azlan, Jacqui, Joshua and Julia all had the right to life. It is God's will that you are here. Not just to be here, but He has a purpose for your lives. I pray that each of you will seek His face to learn and fulfill *His* purpose. I love each and every one of you, as I have expressed to you time and again.

I also dedicate this book to Mama who is now in heaven with Jesus. The tireless sacrifices she made for me and my siblings were extraordinary. Her remarkable ability to love, nurture and support me throughout my life was supernatural. She trusted God with all of her heart. Her living example has made me who I am. She was the strong beautiful mother I needed. Mama consistently told me that, *through Christ all things are possible.* I live by that truth today.

Finally, I dedicate this book to my brother and sister-in-law, the late Alvin and Margie Smith, who lovingly raised my daughter, Margo. To my brother Jimmy and the late Carolyn Smith who took me in when I had no place else to go. I am eternally grateful.

CHAPTER 1

I Don't Want to Live Anymore

It's 1964 I'm here tonight over the little gas stove in our bathroom. I turn the gas up full blast while inhaling with all of my might. I want to die tonight. I don't want to live to see the disappointment on my mother's face when she finds out I am pregnant. I have let everybody down. I don't want to face anyone. I am seventeen, a senior in high school. In 1964, girls were not allowed to go to school pregnant.

This last year of my life has felt like a ride on the world's most dangerous rollercoaster. I have finally reached the ground and I am extremely dizzy.

We live in Huntington, West Virginia. It's a small town. Even if we don't know everyone's name or have a relationship with them, we all know each other in passing. Most of the African Americans in Huntington live in an area basically from Fourteenth to Twentieth streets and from Seventh Avenue to Eleventh Avenue. We all speak to one another.

Our community is unique in that at one time, African Americans went to Barnett Elementary School and Frederick Douglass Junior and Senior High School. For that reason, many of us felt like family. Most of our sisters, brothers, and parents went to the same schools and were taught by some of the same teachers. It was a pretty close-knit community.

Down the street from where I lived on Sixteenth Street and Third Avenue is Marshall University. Huntington is a college town. Many of the houses in our neighborhood were old wooden frame dwellings. Most dwellings were like our house which needed extensive repairs. There were red cobblestone streets that flooded on my block when there was a heavy rain.

We lived on Tenth Avenue and Sixteenth Street. Mr. Lyons lived on the corner in a little shack. He was in charge of selling ice from the icehouse on that corner. And he raised Billy goats. He also had an old horse. The goats got loose ever so often and chased unsuspecting people down the street. Across Sixteenth Street was the grocery store where my parents had an account sometimes. It was run by a Caucasian gentleman who closed the accounts at his discretion.

Next door to the grocers was the Johnson's Five and Ten Cents Store. We ate so much candy and ice cream there, until some of my teeth rotted. Mr. Johnson owned that store. He was another Caucasian man, and I know he made a fortune off of all of our families. Across the street from his store was the White Way Laundry and Dry Cleaners. I never really thought about that name until I wrote it in this book. Around the corner from Mr. Johnson's store was the Holiness church that my Great Aunt Josie and Great Uncle Mr. Vaden attended. Next to that church was our own Frederick Douglass High School which the school board closed in 1962 for desegregation. Not integration just desegregation. We never were integrated into the culture of Huntington High School we were instructed to attend. There were clubs and organizations that already existed when we arrived at the school, but most of us couldn't afford to participate. They had dues and rules that left us out. Many of the white students and teachers didn't want us to integrate. They told us they didn't. Thus, the school was desegregated not integrated.

Despite all of the segregation and poverty that some of us experienced, our community was a great place to be raised. The African American adults were very protective of us. To my knowledge, we all got spankings or a better description might be whippings. I deserved everyone I got. There was much love and much discipline. Most of the adults in the community had our parents' permission to speak to us whenever we were out of line. We knew they loved us.

Tall with Blue Eyes

In 1964 this guy walked up to me as I was sitting on my front porch and proceeded to engage me in conversation. He was very good looking; he was tall, had blue eyes and smiled with a big gap between his two front teeth. I thought that gap was cute. I thought he was cute. A tall handsome black dude with blue eyes. I know I was vulnerable and taken in by this guy's good looks and charm. I was vulnerable because my very first boyfriend had recently left me for another girl. That broke my heart.

Let's call this handsome guy, Tim. I think his goal was to get my attention quickly. He was very complimentary, telling me how beautiful I was. No one had ever told me that I was beautiful, not even my Daddy. Most of the time Tim called me Miss Smith giving me the highest respect. I wasn't really interested in him at first, mainly because the little bit I did know about him was not positive.

I think he had dropped out of school in the eighth or ninth grade. I'll just say, we didn't socialize in the same circles. However, both of us were still just kids. He had this boyish air about himself, but he was still very interested in me. He was consistently nice to me and, he even started coming to our youth group at church. That's where we spent much of our time together.

My mother wasn't keen on him dating me mainly because his dad would let him drive his family's car from time to time. She saw that car as a vehicle to get me in trouble and she was right. Nevertheless, we got to know each other pretty quickly. Over time we thought we were deeply in love and so we became inseparable. I didn't know how it was going to work out with him long term, because I knew I was going away to college that next year. I had been accepted to attend Tennessee State College and was extremely excited to go.

Believe me when I tell you that, we were empty headed, caught up with emotions, and we'll think about that tomorrow, teenagers. Nevertheless, we really did think we were in love.

As time went on, I acted as responsibly as I could thus, Mama gave me more and more freedom to go to movies with him and ride in that car. That was a mistake. I was not always truthful with her as to where we were going and certainly not truthful about what we had been doing.

I really fell in love with Tim. There was so much to like about him. He was kind and thoughtful also. His blue eyes were piercing.

We talked to each other about everything. He was always interested in my point of view. Tim actually thought I was smart. No one had ever paid that much attention to me before. We became very close.

One day I realized my menstrual period was late. I was normally right on time with my period. Now, I was concerned but not worried. I missed my period yet, after the month had passed fear gripped me. From that point on it was difficult for me to concentrate. When I told Tim I had missed my period he said, "Good, good girls get married don't they?" Those words devastated me. I was so angry with him for saying that. It made me feel like he *wanted* me to get pregnant. I know he didn't, but that's how I felt. I guess he didn't know or understand that I was afraid, confused and so ashamed of myself.

After missing my period, I wasn't sleeping at night. I was so sad; I couldn't concentrate at school and I didn't know what I was going to do. I was full of fear. My thoughts were consumed with what am I going to do? I was angry with Tim, so I didn't want to talk to him. I had to figure this thing out. I knew Mama was going to suspect something at some point, but I couldn't tell her. This would be a great disappointment to her, and I never wanted to disappoint Mama. It wasn't that Mama was a tyrant or mean to me, she loved me and I knew it. She just wanted so much *more* for me than she had. She had told me to keep my dress down, and I could do and be anything I wanted to be in life. For me to have been accepted to college meant as much to her as it did to me. My brother Willie and his wife Gerry were going to help me go to college and Mama was thankful for that. Now I was pregnant. What am I going to do?

CHAPTER 2

Fear Was the Darkroom Where Satan Developed My Negatives

Most days I was moping around so exhausted and sad. I had very little to say to anyone, just answering yes and no to their questions.

About a week after I had missed my period, I was washing dishes and Mama came in the kitchen.

She said, "I haven't seen anything upstairs in the bathroom trash can this month. It would be a shame if you had to marry that boy." Then she left the house.

My heart sank and began to pound like a big bass drum. I never turned around or said a word. I knew for certain that she knew I was pregnant. I thought, *Oh God!*

I had been so stressed out about missing my period, I had forgotten to ask Mama for fifty cents to get me some sanitary napkins. That would have given me time to figure out a solution to my crisis. That huge oversight gave me away for sure. I dried my hands then ran upstairs to the bathroom.

That is why I don't want to live any longer. I turned on that old gas stove by the toilet, started inhaling over and over, deeper and deeper, trying to die. I don't know how long I had been doing that when suddenly, the Lord God Almighty spoke to me,

> *"You call yourself a Christian and you can't trust* Me *to see you through this?"*

Wow. To my knowledge God had never spoken to me like that before. Somehow, I knew it was Him. His voice and words literally permeated my whole being getting my full attention. I thought to myself, God is speaking to me and trying to save my life. That is amazing. As simple as those words were, it dawned on me, *I am a Christian, I do love God and He does love me.* This was my proof that God's promises are true and He can be trusted to fulfill them. For He (God) Himself has said,

> I will not in any way fail you nor give you up nor leave you without support. I will not I will not. I will not in any degree leave you helpless (relax My hold on you)! Assuredly not! (Hebrews 13:5b AMP)

The Word of God at that moment cut through all of my faulty deadly thinking.

> The Word of God is quick powerful and sharper than any two-edged sword, piercing even to the dividing asunder of soul and spirit, and of the joints and marrow, and is a discerner of the thoughts and intents of the heart. (Hebrews 4:12)

God knew I was operating in fear and out of my flesh. However, the intent of my heart was to kill myself, but I Praise God He did not allow that to happen. I had resorted to a permanent solution for a temporary challenge. Thankfully, God is faithful even when we are not. Thankfully that was only the beginning of this story.

CHAPTER 3

What Was I Thinking?

I'VE LEARNED THAT GOD has a call or assignment for every person's life. Yes, God has a purpose for us all. That's why Satan tries to cut us off at an early age because he hates God. His strategy is to get us completely diverted from the plan God has for our lives, and move us into areas of distraction and destruction. There was and is a call on my life as well as a call on my baby's life. Even writing this book is a very important assignment. This is my testimony of God's Faithfulness.

> A significant Scripture that has encouraged and nurtured me in my spiritual growth is that God said, "Before I formed you in the womb I knew and approved of you as My chosen instrument, and before you were born I separated and set you apart, consecrating you; I appointed you as a prophet to the nations." (Jeremiah 1:5 AMP)

I realize that God was talking to Jeremiah, but these words prove to me that unborn children are assigned a purpose even before they get here. God puts into every little baby in the womb, gifts and talents that they will develop as they grow. I also believe that

God gets us here however He can. No life is without significance and life begins at conception. Otherwise that life would never grow. Our God is an Awesome God and Father.

Slowly I turned off the stove. Immediately, I heard my brother George downstairs in the front room of the house yell, "Gas!" I had been locked in that bathroom upstairs in the back of the house for I don't know how long. I wasn't even dizzy and didn't have a headache, but the house had filled with gas as Mama and George came in the front door downstairs. She had only been gone approximately thirty minutes. It amazed me to realize that God had protected me and my baby from myself and the devil. Yet, Satan's plan was to kill me and my baby.

I opened the bathroom door and walked out. Mama met me and hugged me tightly and asked, "What are you doing? What is wrong with you? We will work through this. It will be all right." I knew for sure then that she knew I was pregnant. I broke down and began to weep, cry and sob uncontrollably. I had never cried like that before in my life. I literally could not stop crying. I finally released on Mama's shoulder all of the fear and anxiety I had held for the last several weeks.

Mama and George panicked. They didn't know what to do. Mama called our Pastor Rev. Smith who came right over. I think it was about 8:00 p.m. I don't remember exactly. Rev. Smith took me into the Livingroom trying to calm me down and he finally got me to stop crying. He asked me if I were pregnant. I told him yes. He asked, "Who is the father?" I told him Tim, which he already knew because we both were in the youth group at the church where he pastored. He knew that we were dating. Tim lived next door to Rev. Smith. I was so embarrassed to admit to him that I was pregnant because he was like a father figure to me. I had so much respect for him, and I know I disappointed him also. I started crying again and he said, "Jackie it will be okay. You will be all right, but you have to pull yourself together. Go in the kitchen, tell your Mother you are pregnant and ask her to please help you."

"Oh no I can't tell her Rev. Smith. I just can't tell her. I have already broken her heart and disappointed her. I know she can't bear to hear anything else from me. I just can't tell her."

Of course she and my brother could hear every word we were saying. The rooms were only a few steps apart. Rev. Smith insisted, "Yes you can Jackie, you must." He finally got me up off the sofa to go into the kitchen, where Mama and George were waiting for me. I walked slowly, hesitantly almost not able to put one foot in front of the other. I looked into Mama's eyes that were red from crying. Her face was flushed.

"Mama," I said, and I broke down again. She hugged me as we both cried. "I'm so sorry Mama please help me."

"It's going to be all right Jackie." I could see the fear in her eyes. She really didn't know what to say or what to think. I'm sure she was traumatized first by my suicide attempt. Traumatized even more when she learned that her seventeen year old daughter, who hadn't graduated high school yet, was pregnant.

I couldn't talk anymore, so they didn't pressure me to say anything else that night. I just sat in the living room while Rev. Smith counseled me. He said to me, "You have to trust God, Jackie, to show you what to do." I remember him quoting to me from the spiritual hymn, "Beneath the Cross of Jesus." Some of the words I remember are:

Beneath the cross of Jesus I find a place to stand,

and wonder at such mercy that calls me as I am;

for hands that should discard me hold wounds which tell me, "Come."

Beneath the cross of Jesus my unworthy soul is won.

That song became a great comfort to me in months to come. As comforting as that was, the one thing that all four of us feared was what Daddy was going to say or do. You never knew about Daddy. Sometimes he would snap and be angry about the least little thing. My pregnancy was no little thing. All of us knew what his reaction *could* be, because all of us knew him including Rev. Smith.

I went to bed that night more troubled than I'd ever been. I did not sleep at all that night and I know Mama didn't either. Neither did I sleep well any night after that. I had opened the door to the spirit of fear. I was truly afraid for me, Mama and my baby. 1John 4:18 says fear has torment. That word torment is translated in the Greek: Punishment, penal inflection, to curtail and to chastise. I was being tormented in my mind. Thoughts of shame and guilt raced through my head nonstop. It was so painful that my heart would race with anxiety all through the night. I cried and continued to beg God to help me. The other overwhelming emotion was the shame. When you are going to have a baby, everybody knows what you did to get pregnant. As I stated before, in the small town of Huntington in 1964 where we lived, most of the African Americans knew one another. I dreaded to think of the ridicule my parents would have to endure. Gossip about me would most likely take place on almost every front porch in our neighborhood. It had always been like that in the past. I think in any small town, there was usually talk about the girls who got pregnant before marriage. I would be no exception.

Before I became pregnant, my life was great. I had the world's greatest Mama and family. My mother loved all nine of us and made us all feel like each of us was an only child. Well, that was my perception anyway. I was the eighth of the nine children and the baby girl, so that might have influenced the way I saw things. In the nineteen fifties and sixties, Huntington was the perfect place to raise a family. For many years we went to an all-black elementary, junior and senior high schools. Barnett Elementary, and Frederick Douglass High School, which was a junior and senior high school combined. We knew all the African American teachers and they all knew us well. Many of those teachers had taught some of our parents. They had taught at least seven of my siblings. Those teachers knew our potential and demanded that we reach it. There was no doubt in our minds that they loved us and genuinely cared about our futures.

Our teachers worked so closely with us that I actually knew the smell of some of their perfume and the male teachers their cologne. If we failed to complete an assignment, or needed extra help on something, we were told to come to their home to finish the work. Our teachers were part of our community and some of them went to church with us.

Desegregation Not Integration

Sadly, and much to my disappointment in 1961, the State Board of Education closed our Frederick Douglass High School. The purpose was integration. It turned out not to be integration but desegregation. We were not integrated into Huntington High School because we became the minority in every classroom in that school. We had no ability to truly integrate with equality into any social workings of that school. I was crushed at that decision to close our school. I remember that day vividly. I was in bed and Mama woke me up and showed me the newspaper headline, "Douglass High School Closed." I stayed in bed the rest of the day.

I was a majorette in the band at Frederick Douglass when they closed our school doors. We were forced to go to the mostly Caucasian, Huntington High school. The band director told me, "There will be no black legs marching in front of *this* band." He wouldn't let me try out for a majorette position. That was humiliating.

Our intelligent, more than qualified school teachers from Douglass could only get teaching positions in grade schools or junior high schools. I think that was true for all of them except one teacher. I was devastated. We tried to adjust but it was very difficult for me and many others. Some of my close friends never made the adjustment and dropped out of school.

Even with segregation, growing up in Huntington was enriching and secure. Some families didn't even lock our doors in our neighborhood. Our house could be opened with a skeleton key if we did lock the door. You could buy those keys at the five and ten cent store down the street. I never heard of any home being vandalized. I have always loved my hometown and the way I was raised. We had a productive and promising childhood with much love, good people, and lots of encouragement in our neighborhood.

Happy and Fun Loving

I was called silly by many of my friends. I was happy, fun loving and always tried to get along with everyone. Most of the time I had no reason to be sad. I found something funny or fun in everything I did. My friend Emma Scott lived two doors down from my house. We would sit on her front porch late at night and laugh and talk for hours. Our families were close friends. There seemed to always be something to laugh about.

Yet after going through the desegregation process of our schools, I was traumatized. I became more sober minded rather than silly. For the first time in my life I was made to feel less than. It seemed every day was some kind of fight about something in school. I just wasn't used to that struggle. Nevertheless, we had come through that era adjusting fairly well on the surface. I say on the surface because one of the white teachers in the white school asked me, "What trade are you interested in? I really don't think you are college material." Her statement was meant to demean me. After that, my World History teacher had told me, "I'm not answering any of your questions, we don't want you down here so you either get it or you don't."

I was crushed. That's what I mean when I say, I was *traumatized*.

"I didn't know what they were talking about." Of course, all of this was said before I knew I was accepted at Tennessee State College. Now learning that I was pregnant, I couldn't begin to think what my future would look like.

It is difficult for me to fully convey to you the dreams and high hopes Mama had for me. She often encouraged me and told me I could do all things through Christ who strengthens me. (Philippians 4:13) She prayed that I would not get caught in the traps of the devil. We laughed a lot together. She was so much fun. We often talked about what I wanted to do in life. I would tell her I'm going to be a singer like Dianna Ross and the Supremes, or I'm going to be a nurse I'll go to nursing school. I think I'm going to be an actress on television. Yes, I was like any other silly teenager, I didn't have a clue. Mama would look at me and say, "An empty wagon makes a lot of noise coming down the road." I had to figure out what that meant. Her translation was, "Just Do It!"

Mama and I were very close. She was strict with us but playful at the same time. She would get in the living room and dance with Michael my brother and me. She was never a person to talk about people, not a gossiper. Mama was kind-hearted, wise, soft spoken while smiling most of the time. She would say some of the funniest things to make us laugh.

I remember sitting in First Baptist Church one Sunday. The choir had finished singing, Reverend Smith was preaching while folks were saying, "Amen, preach brother." Mama leaned over to me, like she was looking for something then said, "The aftershave lotion that man is wearing in front of us is so loud, I can hardly hear the preacher." She never cracked a smile, but I thought I would fall off the pew laughing silently. She told me one day in the grocery store, "That lady's titties are so big they look like two cocked pistols." I almost didn't recover from that one because that is exactly what they looked like. I enjoyed being with her. I loved my Mama and I needed her. And I needed so much more than just her fun wit. I needed her wisdom.

To know my mother was to love her. Some people didn't understand her because she was a quiet person to outsiders, she didn't talk very much at all. She was not a social butterfly. She was almost ignored in many society circles. Lillie Smith grew up on a farm in Bedford, Virginia one of twelve children. She only went to the fourth grade. She had to work to help feed the family, however she could. That's one reason she was so excited about my going to College. She told me that when she was a child she worked for this, old white lady, just to be paid in eggs. She recalled how she was gathering the eggs from the chickens and the lady said, "You don't know how to gather no eggs." She snatched them out of Mama's hands, put them in her apron started to walk toward the house, stumbled and fell on the eggs and broke them. And when Mama snickered, she beat Mama.

She had a very hard and lean life. She wanted to have a better life. I guess that is why she met and married my Daddy as a young lady and began to have children soon after they married. Nine children to be exact. As a result of that early marriage, she did without so much most of her life. We were very poor. Some people say they were poor growing up, but they didn't know it. Well, I knew it. I could see so many others close to us in our community who had much more than we did, like food in their refrigerators. When I was growing up we called them iceboxes. An icebox was a refrigerator that used a block of ice in the top or bottom to cool the food. As a child, I never remember us going grocery shopping. We went to the store and got one or two things at a time. First of all, Mama and Daddy never had a car. We walked everywhere. Did you ever see the movie, *The Help?* Mama *was* the help. When I was a little girl, Daddy worked in the coal mines in southern West Virginia. It was better known as the coal fields, but we lived in Huntington. Our town was right on the Ohio River approximately 250 miles from Columbus, Ohio. The reason I want you to know more about Mama is because she is my *shero. She is the *shero of this story, the *feminine hero of my life. Many people have a close bond with their mothers as I did, however, our relationship was truly a soul tie. Most times good but sometimes unhealthy.

Now before your mind starts racing in the wrong direction, let me explain what I mean by unhealthy. As the youngest girl, there was just my little brother and I left at home after my older siblings had gone. Mama shared a lot with me. I also observed maybe more than she wanted me to see in her struggle to take care of us. I saw how hard she worked day after day. Often when she returned home, she had pain in her back, her legs and feet. She soaked her feet in a pan of water while she tried to catch her breath. I dried her feet with a towel. Looking at her feet caused me pain. They had corns and callouses and two big bunions. Her feet changed into that state from years of wearing old cheap run over shoes, some of those shoes she got from the rummage sale on the corner. That was all she could afford to buy. During one period of time when I was in grade school, I remember Mama had two pairs of shoes, one pair she wore to church, and another were also run over and a beat up pair she worked in. Sometimes she wore old cut-out tennis shoes, and I don't mean Nike's. Neither pair were fit to wear at all, but that was what she had.

I spent most of my time with Mama and sympathized with all she was going through. She worked so hard for just a little bit of money and tried to stretch that bit to feed us. Trying to make all the ends meet took a great toll on her spirit, soul and body. I remember sitting on our front porch in Huntington praying for

Mama and asking God to send a white person by our house to give her some money. As a little girl I thought only white people had a lot of money. I felt so sorry for Mama.

We went to the rummage sale regularly. There was one down the street and around the corner from us. I don't know who owned those rummage establishments. Because I always wanted to help Mama, when I was a little girl, my uncle Herman gave me a quarter. I went to the rummage sale and bought Mama an old white dingy fur coat. She laughed and told me don't be wasting any more money like that. On Mother's Day one year, she was in bed not feeling well, which was so rare. I felt bad for her. To cheer her up, I found a picture of one of my older brother's old girlfriends, wrapped it up in newspaper and gave it to her for Mother's Day. I chose that picture because the girl was so pretty. Her name was Betty Joyce McClain. Mama thanked me and laughed and cried at the same time. I loved Mama so much. I think I learned co-dependency as a child. That was the unhealthy part. I wanted to please Mama because she had so few pleasing events in her life from my perspective. I wanted to make her happy.

CHAPTER 4

Save the Children

WHILE WE ARE YOUNG the enemy tries to cut us off from our destiny early; he will do so, however he can. That is what was happening to me. I just didn't know at that time that, "The thief comes only in order to steal, kill and destroy. Jesus said, I came that they may have and enjoy life, and have it in abundance to the full, until it overflows." (John 10:10 AMP) Many young people are cut off in the prime of their lives and are never able to recover. They encounter obstacles, catastrophes or devastating events at an early age because that is how Satan operates. He goes after the young and spiritually uninformed. Some situations can cause severe disappointment hurt and depression. Often people go through their adult lives dealing with bouts of depression as a result of something that happened to them in their childhood. That is the devil's strategy. Sadly, that's what happened to me. The saving Grace about my attempting suicide was that I had been taught about Jesus Christ. I had asked Him to come into my heart at age seven. He did and He was able to get my attention in the nick of time. He only had to remind me that He had died for me so that I didn't have to die. That is what so many young people don't know or they are so hurt they don't want to know.

Christ died and rose again paying for our sins, dumb mistakes and even deliberate mess-ups with His blood. He died for the sins we have committed and those we will commit in the future. If we just receive Him and His forgiveness and repent, we can benefit and heal. Many people don't believe that, but I do.

God made the way to salvation as simple as He possibly could.

> **If thou shalt confess with thy mouth the Lord Jesus, and shalt believe in thine heart that God raised Him from the dead, thou shalt be saved. For with the heart man believeth unto righteousness; and with the mouth confession is made unto salvation.**
>
> **(Romans 10:9-10 KJV)**

I made that confession at seven years old and I meant it. God stopped me the night that I tried to commit suicide from killing my babies, grandbabies present and future. He saved me from aborting my destiny. Abortion is contrary to the will of God.

There is a song by the gospel singer Anthony Brown that says,

> *He thought I was worth saving, so He came and changed my life.*
>
> *He thought I was worth keeping, so He cleaned me up inside.*
>
> *He thought I was to die for, so He sacrificed His life."*

That is why I am going to tell everyone I know about Jesus Christ and what He has done for me. I am forever grateful to Him for

His eternal sacrifice. His sacrifice was made for you also, you only have to receive Him. You can do that right now.

At the time of my attempted suicide, I wasn't really thinking about aborting my future or my babies. I was just trying to escape the horrific pain my flesh was experiencing. I have learned so much since then. Inside of me was the first born that would open my womb. The first born of any mother is always a very important seed. That first born opens the womb so that other births can take place if you so desire and I did. There are things that God wants to be birthed into the earth that He reveals to us as we go along. This baby that I almost killed, turned out to be one of great importance to me and to her biological father.

CHAPTER 5

What Would Daddy Say?

My and Mama's greatest fear was what would Daddy say about my pregnancy. The day came when we found out what Daddy said and what he did. It was *not a good day.* On that day thankfully, my brother George and Mama were there to protect me. While we were all in the same room, Mama said, "Willie, Jackie is going to have a baby."

I was sitting down in a chair in the middle room and he lunged at me. My brother George intervened and grabbed him. He was much more furious than I had imagined. He was enraged at both me and Mama. He turned to her, "This is all your fault," he yelled. He always blamed Mama for everything. If our dog Tippy turned over his water, he yelled at Mama. He was just an angry man. He must have been raised in an angry household, I don't know why he was angry. So when he learned about my pregnancy he said some very hurtful things to me that I won't repeat. He called me horrible names that he knew were not true. He didn't use any profanity, although I felt like I had been cursed. I don't know what would have happened if George hadn't been there. All of the name calling and yelling was terrible enough, but the worst came when he said,

"You will never bring a baby in this house!" What did he say?

I was already crying uncontrollably, consequently, I didn't think I heard him correctly. What? I was taken aback. What did that mean? Can't bring my baby in this house? In all of my thinking about what I was going to do, this thought never crossed my mind. Now I questioned what I would *really* do and where I would go? I weep even as I write these words, because writing this book is another layer of healing that I am experiencing by the power of the Holy Spirit. Did his words mean I was going to be put out of my house, was he disowning me? I thought all of this to myself because I was afraid to say a word. "Although my father and my mother have forsaken me, yet the Lord will take me up (adopt me as His child)." (Psalms 27:10 KJV) That is exactly what God did, He adopted me as his child. I kept hearing in my mind, *you have to forgive him, you have to forgive him.* I want you to know right now before I go any further, that I forgave my daddy soon after that day for everything. As a matter of fact I forgave him before I had my baby. When I was a young child Mama taught me that I must forgive people quickly or Jesus won't forgive my sins.

> **Whenever you stand praying, if you have anything against anyone forgive him and let it drop, leave it, let it go, in order that your Father who is in heaven may also forgive you, your own failings and shortcomings and let them drop. But if you do not forgive, neither will your Father in heaven forgive your failings and shortcomings.**
> **(Mark 11:25-26 AMP)**

I began to cry as I wrote those words. I have realized that there are times you *can* forgive a person overall then move on. On the other hand, we often never forgave them for specific words that wounded us. You might be carrying around little foxes that may be spoiling your vine. I continue to pray today,

> Search me Oh God and know my heart; try me and know my thoughts: And see if there be any wicked way in me, and lead me in the way everlasting. (Psalm 139:23-24)

There are some things I find that God Himself has to bring to the surface of our hearts that we may have overlooked for years. I believe this is the process John speaks of in the Bible:

> If we confess our sins He [God] is faithful and just to forgive our sins, and to cleanse us from all unrighteousness.
> (1 John 1:9 emphasis added)

I know now that the cleansing process takes some of us longer than others. I don't mind that at all as long as I get cleansed.

When I began to weep while writing about forgiveness, I implored God, "Father I forgive my Daddy for saying those specific words to me that hurt me so deeply. His words made me feel abandoned and worthless at that moment. I repent and ask you to forgive me for holding that offense for so long. I put it under the Blood of Jesus."

While writing this book I was cleansed a little bit more. That is why I had to put it under the blood of Jesus. He poured out His blood for the forgiveness of our sins at the cross. In short, the blood still works.

CHAPTER 6

What About Tim?

You might be wondering what my boyfriend, the father of my unborn child was saying about all of the mayhem that was taking place. As I said earlier, when I told him weeks before that I had missed my period he said, "Good, good girls get married don't they?" I didn't want to assume that I knew exactly what Tim meant when he spoke those words. But I understood them to mean that I had no other choice but to marry him. After what Daddy said to me, I thought that marrying him *was* the only decent thing to do. Yet deep in my heart, something didn't feel right about getting married just because I was pregnant.

Looking back now, I realize that we were just kids but we had done an adult thing. I knew nothing about my body. I didn't know about male ejaculation and female eggs being fertilized or any other facts about sexual reproduction. Maybe our teachers explained the facts of life to us in Home Economics class, but I wasn't listening. Maybe I thought sexual reproduction didn't pertain to me, or maybe I was absent that day. Who knows?

Both Tim and I did think we were passionately in love. We were teenagers hopelessly caught up in our emotions? I knew two things for sure, Tim wanted desperately to marry me, and he wanted his baby. Of course there were a few obstacles. He had quit school in the eighth or ninth grade, and was working as a bell-hop at a downtown hotel, yet he lived with his parents who had no room for us. We had nowhere to go, nor anything to sustain us or our baby, and neither of our parents were financially able to help us at all. My parents certainly couldn't help us financially even if they wanted to. My Daddy had only gone to the sixth grade. He worked for years as a coal miner, and contracted Silicosis. Hence, he was laid off from the coal mines years earlier and had no pension. He eventually had to have one of his lungs removed. At the time of my pregnancy, he was a night watchman at a restaurant making forty dollars a week. I might also mention this same restaurant did not serve black people and Daddy had to go through the back door to even work there. It was a different day in time.

My Mama, bless her heart, had only gone to the fourth grade. When I was very young, she worked as an elevator operator at a downtown hotel. I don't know what she was paid, but we never had extra money. Now she worked as a maid in private homes.

I told you that my parents never owned a car, and I wish Tim's parents had never owned one either. That's where I got pregnant in that red and white Ford. His parents were probably in the same shape financially as mine. There was no one to help us. God *had* to come through for us.

Tim loved and wanted me and his baby desperately. This little baby was wanted and loved so much by both of us. All we were trying to do was figure out how to feed, clothe and keep our baby. Honestly, the thought of abortion never crossed our minds. We had done some dumb stuff, but abortion was not going to be added to our list of bad choices. That was never an option. Furthermore, I don't think I had ever even heard the term abortion at that time in my life. I knew one girl who told me that she had gotten a shot that started her period, but I don't know if that meant that she was really pregnant or not. I also don't know what kind of shot that was, nor did I ask. When I think of abortion, I believe it is destroying what only God could create. Killing what *only* God has brought to life. The Bible states that *we are fearfully and wonderfully made.* Only God could do that, and I respect and honor His creation.

Tim took my mom and me to my first doctor's appointment to make sure I was pregnant, and he paid for the visit. The clinic was at this little hospital in the west end of town. I don't know why we went to that particular hospital. Maybe it was the cheapest or maybe we chose it to avoid running into people we knew. That red building may have been a hospital where people went who were on government assistance. I don't know. All I remember is that it was the darkest most depressing looking place I had ever seen. I never went back there again.

The doctor said I was approximately six or seven weeks pregnant so that was that, he confirmed the pregnancy. Neither of us had any insurance or money to pay for medical bills. I had only been to a doctor myself maybe five times in my entire life because of the lack of finances. I had had a hernia operation, a sleigh ride accident and was hospitalized for a week. I don't know who paid for that. I'd gotten spider bites at 4-H Camp. That was the extent of my medical history. From the depths of my heart, I know that Tim did everything he could to prove to me that he would be a good father. The sad part was that he didn't have much money to work with at the time. Despite all of these realities, I was going to marry him anyway. I did love him; plus it was, *the right thing to do.*

CHAPTER 7

Stop the Wedding!

Despite the pregnancy, mama hadn't pressured me asking whether or not Tim and I were going to get married. We still saw each other frequently while I was trying to keep up a good front at school. One night after finishing my homework, I was watching television with Mama. Something funny happened on the program we were watching. We laughed together then she turned to me quickly and said, "I think if you get married now, it will be the end of your life." I perceived when she spoke those words, that she had been holding them inside for a while. However, I knew exactly what she meant. She wasn't saying I would physically die, rather she inferred that all of my hopes, dreams, ambitions and potential might get lost and never be fulfilled.

"What?" I said, "You don't want me to get married? I thought that was *the right thing to do.*"

She looked directly in my eyes with compassion and answered, "You don't know what being married is all about." I just don't think that is what you should do right now. I don't think you have thought this through."

I was stunned to hear her say, "I don't think you should get married." I was trying to make things look and be a little more respectable for her and Daddy in this small-town environment. I realized, after I thought about it that I was full of guilt about my sexual activity. The shame factor and my lack of sleep clouded my thinking. There again, I was trying to please Mama. I didn't say anymore to her, and she didn't say anything else to me that night. I headed to bed. I prayed about what she had said to me, and prayed some more the next day. I continued to pray and by the grace of God, having all the facts laid out more clearly in front of me, I made a decision.

Since I had disobeyed Mama's wisdom in the past when she told me to keep my dress down, I knew I should obey her wisdom now and not rush into marriage. It became very clear to me over night that I had more to think about than myself. I had to consider the welfare of my baby.

Mama was correct when she said, I knew nothing about what marriage and its responsibilities involved. Besides that, how and where would we live? I just wanted to keep my baby. Of course when I told Tim that I was not going to marry him, he got in my face saying,

"Yes you will marry me. You know that I love you. I want to take care of you and my baby."

"I know you do, but how?" He was furious, I then saw a side of him I hadn't seen before. I had never seen Tim angry at me.

He said sternly, "There is no way you will keep my baby from me. I will get my baby and I will get you." Not surprisingly fear gripped me again. This time it was fear of Tim. I wasn't really afraid that Tim would hurt me physically, but I was afraid of what he might do in this angry state. I had no idea what he could do, and I don't think he did either. I just didn't want to cause my family any more grief.

Meanwhile, I was still trying to get through my senior year of high school without anyone knowing I was pregnant. In 1964 a girl could not go to school and be pregnant. My every waking thought was that I had to at least finish high school. Even though I was accepted to college, I couldn't go now. That was a great disappointment to me and my family. I felt like I had let the whole world down and that included myself.

It disturbed me greatly that my relationship with Tim was fractured. I was still in love with him regardless of the difficult circumstances. Moreover, I had to make some mature decisions. Those decisions were necessary for the health and welfare of our baby. I had more to think about than myself.

CHAPTER 8

Pregnancy And The Great Pretender

I WAS GOING TO SCHOOL every day but could barely keep my eyes open now. I stayed so sleepy and hungry during the day. Yet, I was blessed never to have had morning sickness.

My routine was to rush into the classroom, get my work done, and lay my head on the desk and go to sleep. When that school year began I was an "*A-B*" student. That is why I was accepted to college. By the end of the school year which was the end of May, I went from a "B" in chemistry to a "D" and was glad to get that. My chemistry teacher was baffled. Mrs. Marples said, "Jackie I don't know what has happened to you; is there something wrong at home? You are not the same student. It's like your mind is somewhere else." I told her I just couldn't concentrate. I was able to maintain my other grades. Thankfully, I had more than enough credits to graduate going into my senior year. I took chemistry as a challenge or a dare from the boyfriend who had broken up with me before I met Tim. He said I couldn't do it, but I proved him wrong. Once I applied myself, I enjoyed chemistry until my pregnancy made me sleepy. Plus my mind was in a knot.

Those next four months before graduation, I felt like my feet were in cement blocks. I had to push my way through every day. People were whispering. I noticed a couple of my friends looking at my stomach. I had to smile, lift my head up and keep moving forward. I kept hearing Mama's voice in my head saying, "Everything is going to be all right."

My Pastor Rev. Smith had counseled me. He and Mrs. Smith, were very kind and caring to me. They knew I needed all the help I could get. Mrs. Smith was a seamstress. To my benefit, 1964 was the year of sack and chemise dresses. Mrs. Smith made some of those waist-less sack dresses for me, and they didn't make me look fat. I am eternally grateful to her until this very day. Ironically her name was Lillie Smith also.

Daily, the question swam around in my head, *"What was I going to do?"* Family members suggested to me many times to adopt my baby out. I rejected this advice at every turn. Those urgings did not come from Mama. If I followed those people's advice, I felt I would go insane wondering where my child was. I would wonder if my baby was in a bad foster home, if my child was being abused. If our child was alive? Was my baby dead? I would not have been able to go on with my life not knowing.

My high school graduation was just a few weeks away when my brother Jimmy in Denver, Colorado called. He and his wife wanted to send me an airplane ticket. They wanted me to come stay with them after graduation until I decided what I was going to do. It seemed like I had been thrown a lifeline. I told them I would love to do that. Mama also thought that was a wonderful idea. Going away might help me to think more clearly.

Tim didn't think my leaving was such a good idea. He was furious. He still wanted me to marry him. Many a night he raced down my cobblestone street in his dad's car. Then he'd put on brakes in front of my house, just to let me know he was out there. I was a nervous wreck. I continued to pray day and night and to ask God to show me what to do. My senior year still hadn't ended.

Graduation was getting closer. Now, all of the senior activities had begun, the prom, the luncheons, the open houses and backyard parties. It wasn't that I wasn't invited. After all, those functions included all of us African American seniors. I was just too ashamed to go. I didn't want to be scrutinized too closely or asked questions that would put me in jeopardy of not graduating. People were definitely talking but not to my face. Everybody tried to act normal around me. More pretense. I had many friends and I think most of them were sad to know I was pregnant and hoped the best for me. It was also sad for me because we were not used to being phony with each other. We loved each other. Unfortunately, I think there were some who *were* comfortable talking about people and carrying the gossip. I still loved them anyway.

Finally graduation day came, the final ceremony we had all been looking forward to and working toward. Mama bought me a real nice straight white dress with a sailor collar trimmed in navy blue. She also bought me some white shoes that hurt my feet terribly. I can see those pointed-toe shoes now. Mama actually went in debt trying to get me through school. When they called my name and I walked across that stage, everybody cheered loudly and clapped their hands, even my teachers. I knew then that they all *knew* and were glad I had made it. My friend Agnes Patrick told me years later, that my close friends were all holding their breath for me. They wanted to see me get my diploma. I cried like a baby when I walked off the stage, but afterward we all rallied around each other taking pictures together. That was one of the happiest days of my life. The relief and release was palpable.

I praised God for taking me across that finish line. It was very difficult; I was four months pregnant, but I was able to graduate high school only by the Grace of God. Being able to graduate meant a lot to me and Mama also. It is still difficult to put into words the pain and anguish we both experienced. It bonded us forever.

Mama was particularly kind to me. She went into debt and bought me a Bulova watch with a beautiful scarab watchband that cost her about seventy dollars. That was a lot of money in those days. It was especially expensive for someone who worked as a maid and housekeeper. It was a tremendous sacrifice. She didn't have to do that, nonetheless, she wanted to let me know she was proud of me for finishing, and she wanted to encourage me to go on. I thank God for the mother He gave to me. She was exactly who I needed. There is a song, *"You're the best thing I never knew I needed"* by NeYo. That's how I feel about Mama.

Lillie's Lines

Mama was a special kind of person. Most people didn't know her like I did. Even some of my older siblings didn't have the same relationship as she and I did. Mama was, in the truest sense of the word, "*old school.*" She had one liners for almost every situation when we were growing up. I refer to them as, *Lillie's lines.*

Allow me to share with you just a few of those idioms. One of Lillie's lines was, "You don't have to go around Jake's barn and get kicked by the mule. I've been back there and he is still kickin'." What she was teaching us was; just listen to my advice and you don't have to suffer the consequences.

Another gem with the same meaning as Jake's barn was, "A hard head makes a soft behind." Also, "I think you have that shirt on hind ponce before." Meaning the shirt is on backwards. "Wow, "You're sitin' mighty high." This meant your skirt is too short for the way you're sitting. Mama also would say when we were getting close to a deadline, "Well, it won't be long as it's been bein". The last *Lilli's line* I will share with you is, "Folks dying ain't never died before." I think that idiom is self-explanatory. (Those are just a few of *Lillie's lines*). She was a delightful person.

I find myself speaking these same words in my everyday interactions. Yes, Lillie Smith was a most unique and God fearing woman. My memories of our times together are golden.

CHAPTER 9

Soul Ties and Suffering

Growing up I was very close to my sister Bernice. Out of the nine of us she was the sixth but she was eight years older than me. She was a loving big sister to me who gave me special attention. Bernice combed my hair especially after it was washed. That was a difficult job because my hair was long and very thick. We'd watch television together and she helped me with my homework. Bernice sang in the choir at church and I thought she was the best singer in that choir. Many times Mama made her take me with her when she went to the movies or to cheerleader practice whether she wanted me to tag along or not. I admired her and I thought she was cute.

I wanted to go to see Bernice before I went to Denver to stay with my brother Jimmy. I knew that once I went to Denver, I might not see her for a long time. I was right about that. When I graduated high school she lived in Youngstown Ohio. I felt somewhat of a further kinship to her because she and my Daddy didn't get along well either. Maybe I was looking for some sympathy from her for the way I'd been treated by him. Perhaps I was inviting her to my pity party. She was glad to come. I got that sympathy and love from her when I went to Youngstown. Bernice hugged and assured me before I left her that I would be fine. She said, "Daddy will get over this, that's just the way he is." I agreed and felt much better. I'm glad I got to see my sister. Going there to see her encouraged me to keep my head up and move forward.

Sadly, on the bus ride back from Ohio, I became quite ill. It was a combination of morning and motion sickness on the Greyhound bus I was riding. I felt like I had thrown up the baby. I remember calling Mama at one of the bus stops. I was crying hard. I sobbed, "Mama I am sick, nauseated and don't know if I can make it home. If I die before I get there, just know that I love you and I'm sorry I put you through all of this."

Mama said, "Shut up, and get back on that bus. Pray and come home." I did just that and obviously I did not die. The remaining ride was almost unbearable but I survived it. When I got back to West Virginia, I recuperated for a few days before flying to Denver. Even though I was so sick on the ride home from Youngstown, I am glad I went.

I only told a few people I was going to visit my brother in Denver so there wouldn't be a big scene from Tim. Yet, the reality that I have never expressed to anyone in the past is that I grieved over leaving him also. It is true that we were kids, or teenagers, nonetheless, we really thought we loved each other. For most people there are soul ties that develop especially when you have intercourse with a person. These ties are real and hard to break when you don't know what they are or how to break and destroy them.

I learned years later in my study of the Bible that we are tripartite beings. We are comprised of three parts. God said, "Let us make man in our image after our likeness. (Genesis 1:26) We are a spirit, which is that part of us that is like God, we are made in His image. God is a Spirit and they that worship Him must worship Him in spirit and in truth. (John 4:24) Then we have a soul which is our mind, our will, our emotions and our imagination. And we live in a body, the physical, our earth suit. We also develop soul ties with our parents, close friends, and siblings because they form through our minds our wills and our emotions.

When I left Huntington, I missed Tim deeply. I could never tell my mother or my brothers that. I grieved the breakup of our relationship. After all, Tim was the father of my baby that I was carrying. Tim was the first person to ever tell me I was beautiful. That compliment turned my head. Fathers should be the first one to tell their daughters they are beautiful, but mine had not. I believe fathers can strongly influence their daughters positively by first loving their mothers as Christ loved the church. They also have the opportunity to instill in them by example, Godly values. Fathers can give to their daughters productive ideas that can help them become stable, confident and secure individuals growing up. One of those invaluable ideas is actually telling them that he loves them, and that he will always be there for them. Children always want their father's approval. I was no exception. Just the fact that Tim wanted to marry me and be a father to our baby made me feel special. I missed him terribly and thought so often, *what if?*

I consistently had to reject the feeling that I had been made to leave my home. Being told by my Daddy that I could not bring my baby home left me no other alternative. I was semi-homeless; I had a place to go, but it was not *my* home. I was not ready to leave my childhood home and that hurt.

All of this trauma was happening to a seventeen-year-old girl who had not matured yet. From what I have learned, psychology explains that a teenager's brain doesn't fully develop until age twenty-one. That's one reason I wasn't thinking straight. The mental anguish of all of what I was experiencing and of what was to come, forced me to lean on and look to God in His word to be my strength. But honestly, I didn't know how to do that on my own. I prayed constantly and I know it was the Holy Spirit who directed me to this one passage as I read the Scriptures. I consistently held fast to Psalm 40:

> I waited patiently for the Lord: and He inclined unto me, and heard my cry. He brought me up also out of a horrible pit, out of the miry clay, and set my feet upon a rock, and established my goings. And He hath put a new song in my mouth, even praise unto our God: many shall see it and fear, and shall trust in the Lord. Blessed is that man that maketh the Lord his trust, and respecteth not the proud, nor such as turn aside to lies. Many, O Lord my God, are thy wonderful works which thou hast done, and thy thoughts which are to us-ward: they cannot be reckoned up in order unto thee: if I would declare and speak of them, they are more than can be numbered. Sacrifice and offering thou didst not desire; mine ears hast thou opened: burnt offering and sin offering hast thou not required. Then said I, Lo, I come; in the volume of the book it is written of me. I delight to do thy will, O my God: yea, thy law is within my heart." (Psalm 40:1-8)

I read Psalm 40 over and over and over again until I had it memorized. I also memorized the sixth verse in the Amplified Bible.

You have opened my ears and given me the capacity to hear and obey Your word; Burnt offerings and sin offerings You do not require. (Psalm 40:6 AMP)

I had to believe the Bible and those words kept me from losing my mind. God's word will keep you sane if you believe it.

CHAPTER 10

I Waited Patiently for the Lord

WHEN I GOT TO Denver I was greeted warmly. The good thing about going to Denver was that my brother Jimmy and his wife Bonnie had asked me to come. I was only three years younger than my sister-in-law Bonnie. We had gone to school together. She was head majorette at Frederick Douglass High School when I was a majorette in the ninth grade. My tenth-grade year was when the authorities enforced the Supreme Court's desegregation ruling and closed the school. The traumas in my life were coming more and more frequently.

My brother Jimmy and Bonnie took better care of me than I could have ever expected. They took me to one of the best Ob/Gyn doctors in Denver. They bought me pre-natal vitamins and made sure I ate well. For the first time in my life, I had my own bedroom in this very nice apartment. We went to church most Sundays and God took real good care of me through them.

I also liked Denver. Compared to Huntington it was a big clean city with wide open spaces. Denver was very different from West

Virginia. I felt much better being here in Denver. This relocation gave me a sense of hope. I failed to mention that being at home with my Daddy was emotionally difficult after he found out that I was pregnant. He wouldn't talk to me. Sometimes when I came in a room, he left the room. All of that was painful. But in Denver, the pain began to subside. In Denver things were good. The skies were blue almost every day it seemed. In West Virginia the humidity was usually high and the skies were overcast. Colorado Mountains were like nothing I had ever seen. West Virginia has mountains but compared to the Rockies, they were hills. There are a lot of trees and close together buildings in Huntington that prohibit having a panoramic view of the city. Tenth Avenue where I grew up in West Virginia had cobblestone streets. I didn't see any cobblestone streets in Denver. Denver was beautiful and the air was so clean and fresh.

Jimmy and Bonnie did not let me sit in the corner and feel sorry for myself. Bonnie bought me some nice maternity clothes, not a lot, but enough to last me through the entire pregnancy. They took me to some of the parties and cookouts they were invited to and introduced me to all of their friends. I guess they made me their project. It was a different world. I felt as much at home as possible. In spite of all of this, the burning question in my mind constantly was, what was I going to do? I prayed day and night asking God to talk to me and tell me what to do. I knew in my heart that He would talk to me because He had talked to me that night I tried to kill myself. I was waiting for Him to talk to me again. Although I was in this wonderful place and the baby was growing and healthy, I was homesick. I missed Mama and I still missed Tim.

I cried and prayed every night, but I never really slept well. I felt like time was running out for me to make a decision. I wanted to do what *God* wanted me to do, and I knew that would be the *best* decision for my baby and for me. That is why I continued to pray in faith believing my Father God would instruct me.

I did have one choice, in Alvin. He was one of my older brothers who is the fourth of my eight siblings, who lived in Lansing, Michigan. A month or so earlier he asked if he could adopt my baby. I swiftly told him no I didn't want to do that. My reasoning was that he and his wife argued a lot, and I wanted my baby to have peace. I didn't have the nerve to tell him that, but I think he knew why I said no. He and his wife Margie didn't have any children. My knees were sore from being on them praying every day and night asking for God's instructions. I was now five months pregnant. The baby began to flutter in my womb. That was amazing to me. A real life was taking shape and growing on the inside of me. This was my baby. I began to hold my stomach and tell my baby that we were going to be fine. My body and emotions were going through so many changes. Even though I didn't have an answer yet, I knew I was in a much better place emotionally and physically. Because I believed God and had faith in Him, I had hope. I had favorable and confident expectation as I waited on the Lord. *Wow*! That was so exciting to me.

CHAPTER 11

God Knows My Name!

I CONTINUED TO PRAY DAY and night. I was desperate for God to answer me. One night after getting off of my knees praying, I got into bed. I tried to doze off to sleep when I heard God call my name. "Jackie."

Have you ever had God to call your name? His voice goes to the very core of your being. Think about it, God who created the universe knows our name. I knew it was Him. I had waited five months to hear His voice again. I recognized it at once.

I sat straight up in the bed and said out loud, "Lord let me get up and turn on the light, so no one can tell me I am dreaming." I got out of bed turned on the light, got back in bed and sat up. What I heard wasn't a thundering audible voice but a gentle soothing knowing in my spirit. His voice was in that part of me that is made in His image and His likeness. God is a Spirit and He was speaking to my spirit.

He said to me gently, "Jackie, let your brother Alvin adopt your baby. You will have opposition in this decision, but remember this is *My* will for you and your baby. Tell your brother Alvin that the baby must know that you are the mother as soon as your baby is able to understand. Tell him that you don't want his wife Margie to work and that you want her to stay at home and raise your baby. You will always know where your baby is and can see your baby. Then I want you to go back home to Huntington and start a *new life in Me. You are not giving your baby away, you are leaving your baby with Me. Trust Me.*" Oh my goodness, the heaviness, worry and sadness was lifted from me immediately. I got up walked around the room, crying and praising God and rejoicing quietly. I had finally heard from God. However, it was near midnight, I couldn't wake everyone up with my praising God.

I said, "God please let me know that this is You. I know it is You, but give me some kind of sign. I want to be so sure, that no one can talk me out of this. No matter what."

My heart leapt for joy. Remember I told you I had solidly rejected my brother's offer and the reason for doing so. Now his offer sounded like the very best answer for the love and safety of my baby. I turned off the light, got back in the bed and slept soundly for the first time in five months. Sound sleep was my sign that this was God's will for my baby and me. I woke up in total peace and excitement. I know what *peace that passes all understanding* means. My circumstances had not changed, but I had heard from God and my heart and mind were clear. I also know that Jesus said, "Peace I leave with you: My own peace I now give and bequeath to you. Not as the world gives do I give to you. Do not let your hearts be troubled, neither let them be afraid. Stop allowing yourselves to be agitated and disturbed; and do not permit yourselves to be fearful, intimidated, cowardly and unsettled." (John 14:27 AMP) Wow! That is positively what He left with me, His peace. I have found in my walking with my

Lord Jesus Christ all of these years later, that peace is one of God's greatest benefits. Trust me, I would need it for what was to come.

The very next morning when I told my brother Jimmy and Bonnie, they really didn't think that was a good idea to let Alvin and Margie adopt my baby. But it didn't matter to me, I knew that my decision was God's decision. He told me I would have opposition.

My brother Alvin and his wife Margie were quite excited when I called them. Alvin sent me an airplane ticket, and I left Denver for Michigan that following week. I believe that was part of the urgency I had been feeling. I didn't realize I would have to get on an airplane to fly to Michigan. My doctor advised that, flying on a plane after six months of pregnancy could be risky.

Alvin and Margie lived in a small two bedroom bungalow, so the living quarters were very close. But I still had my own room. It was very small and had just room enough for a full bed pushed against the wall and a small dresser for my clothes. I got along well with them both, but they didn't necessarily get along with each other all the time. There were so many days they argued in the living room. When they argued, I got on my knees in the bedroom and asked God, "Are you sure this is what You want me to do?" He always reassured me that I heard Him clearly, and that I must trust Him all the way. Each time I prayed, He gave me peace.

Once I was settled in Michigan I slept well each night. My baby was growing, moving, kicking. I tried to exercise walking outside whenever the weather permitted. I was very healthy and getting fat. Margie was a good cook. Her greens, okra and tomatoes were my favorites. I loved to feel my baby move on the inside of me. I kept telling my baby that we are in a good place. I had confidence in the doctor they took me to. I don't remember his name right now, but I liked him a lot. My God supplied all of my need according to His riches in glory by Christ Jesus. (Phil. 4:19 KJV) Alvin was more than happy to pay for everything. I was quite familiar with Lansing, Michigan mainly because I had other brothers and sisters who lived there. During many of my childhood summers our family visited my brothers Alvin, George and my two sisters Rosa and Miriam who also lived in Lansing.

When I was about twelve years old, my oldest sister Rosa introduced me to her neighbor Joyce Allen. Joyce was my age, and we became very close friends during those summer visits. We were so close that one Christmas her parents even let her come to Huntington to visit with me. We had big fun. I introduced her to all of my friends. She continues to be a special friend. Her entire family were very loving toward me all of the years we have known one another.

When I went to Lansing pregnant, the Allen family embraced me. They embraced me as family. I desperately needed to hear that they still loved me and didn't condemn me. I still felt like I had disappointed the whole world. Joyce's brother Richard was two years older than we were, so he considered me his little sis. I looked up to Richard. He gave us advice on boys and how boys think. The Allens and I looked forward to being together. I was truly part of this family.

Joyce's mother Mrs. Allen was saved, sanctified and filled with the Holy Spirit. She was a strong woman of God. She was not ashamed of the gospel of Jesus Christ or who she was in Him. I loved her so much. She was a bit full-figured and when she hugged me, it felt real tight and fluffy. Mrs. Allen constantly told us about the Lord and how good He is. She encouraged me to trust the Lord to see me through this pregnancy and beyond. She made sure I had repented and asked the Lord to forgive me for having intercourse outside of marriage. I told her that was one of the first things I did. Not only was she saved, she was an excellent cook. One night she asked me what I wanted to eat. I told her chitterlings. That week she cleaned and cooked me some chitterlings. That was not an easy job, but she wanted to do something special for me.

Mrs. Allen was loud in a good way. Whenever she saw me coming she laughed with a loud voice saying, "Lord, look who has come to town." Then she laughed again and squeezed me.

Joyce's sister Beatrice and their brother Richard and Pops Allen always made fun of my West Virginia accent or twang as they called it. I spent a lot of time with them while I was pregnant. They never condemned me or made me feel ashamed but always welcomed me. God had me covered. The experience of being away from home and from my familiar environment without Mama was painful and traumatic. However, God had positioned certain special souls in my path to lift my spirits. They all helped me to keep my head up and keep moving forward with a smile.

CHAPTER 12

Encourage Yourself
Jackie Smith

THE DAYS OF MY life as a pregnant teenager passed slowly. I continued to look for ways to motivate and encourage myself. I couldn't depend on other people to keep me going and push me along. I tried to remember as many of the good times in my life as I could. I thought that remembering the good times would keep me from being so homesick. The music of the 60's aided me in that endeavor.

Music has always been an exciting and stimulating pleasure of mine. I learned from my band teacher Mr. Simpson, in junior high school that one of the definitions of music is *to make to remember*. Many of us can hear a song and remember what we were doing at that time. Some of us can hear a song, and remember who we were with when that song was popular. The year I conceived my baby, 1964 Motown was really jumping. I spent many of my days enjoying the music coming out of Detroit at that time.

I have always been musically inclined. I thought my singing group might become the next Martha Reeves and the Vandellas, the Marvelettes or the Supremes. I formed a singing group in junior high school that stayed together through high school. We were *The Galaxies.* Our little cluster of stars were Gloria Ritchie, Leslie Smith, better known as Shu Shu, Herma Jean Lewis, Laydia King, Agnes Patrick and myself. We were the best. We performed in all the talent shows singing "Diamonds and Pearls" and an assortment of other artists' songs. We had great fun. My brother George and my sister Bernice who were several years older than me, had singing groups in high school also. They often practiced at our house.

Our house was filled with different kinds of music. I believe that music is in my DNA. Music was in my environment both in and out of school. At Frederick Douglass Junior High School our band director Mr. Simpson taught me how to play the alto and baritone saxophones. I was the only majorette in the band who played an instrument in our spring band concerts that year. Just before they closed Frederick Douglass High School, Mr. Simpson was also teaching me how to play the oboe.

When I was forced to go to Huntington High School, I joined the orchestra and learned to play the violin. We were chosen to participate in the All State Orchestra that year. My singing group, playing musical instruments and performing in talent shows, made me an active and fairly popular teenager. In 1964 Martha Reeves was singing, "*Wait a Minute Mr. Postman.*" I remember that well, because I desperately wanted a letter from anybody at home in Huntington besides Mama.

Even though I was around family in Michigan, I was still lonely. I also missed my friends Shu Shu and Gloria Ritchie; we were known as the three Stooges. I missed the Murrell twins, Linda and Brenda who lived a few houses away from me; we were all very close. All of us had grown up together from nursery school through high school. I missed other friends like Herma Jean, Marvin Spotts, Bobby Murrell, Gene Hayes and Agnes Patrick too. We had a lot in common except, now they were college students and I was becoming a mother. They were pursuing all of the dreams and ambitions we had talked about for years. Together we had imagined what our lives would be like after high school, and how fast we would leave Huntington. Ironically, I did leave Huntington fast, but not the way I had imagined. I had to grow up over the last few months. But, I still wanted to play, sing and be a part of the group. However, there was no more group. Life as I knew it had changed.

CHAPTER 13

It's a Beautiful Girl

My sister-in-law Margie and I enjoyed watching *Peyton Place* on television every week. Margie was a big soap opera fan but Peyton Place was one of her favorite programs. While watching television with Margie I started feeling strange. I had an urge to use the restroom. While in the bathroom I passed a small mixture of blood and mucus in the toilet. I was terrified. Mama had told me that I should never see any blood while pregnant. I told Margie what had happened. She said I should put on a pad and lie down. I called Mama at once. She said, "You're getting ready to have that baby, so lie down, and I will get there as soon as I can. She laughed and said, "It won't be as long as it's been bein'."

I prayed, "Lord don't let me have the baby before Mama gets here. I need her here." I did lie down and slept lightly. I was not having contractions and there was no pain at all. The baby was moving into position and that felt strange but not painful. Alvin and Margie were really on edge and ready to spring into action. I never thought about it then, but Mama must have had her bag packed like she herself was having the baby. She boarded a Greyhound bus and rode approximately four hundred and fifty miles to get to me. She arrived late the next night. Alvin picked her up from the bus station. He was relieved she arrived in time. I was elated to see her; she was happy to see me too.

Alvin put some plastic on my bed to cover part of the mattress just in case the baby surprised us. That night Mama and I lay in the bed together and talked for a long time. She told me all the news from back home and what Daddy was doing and saying. I told her again how sorry I was to have put her through all of this. I glanced her way and saw a tear running down one eye into her hair. Her tear made me cry silently too, because I had disappointed her and I never wanted to. I only wanted to make her proud of me. I silently cried myself to sleep as I had done so many nights prior. I think Mama was also afraid for me knowing the pain I was about to experience. She was correct.

Later that morning at approximately, 4:00 a.m., I was abruptly awakened when my water broke in the bed. I was so afraid when I shook Mama. "Mama, my water broke," I said with my voice shaking. My heart was pounding. I got up quickly went to the bathroom, cleaned up and brushed my teeth. I was holding my legs close together because I thought, maybe the baby might just fall on the floor. Mama do you think the baby will just drop down?

Mama answered, "No, that baby will work its way down, you'll see." Boy did I see. Then Mama said, "We probably should go on to the hospital because you never know with your first baby; they just come whenever they are ready."

Alvin was dressed and ready to drive us to the hospital. Mama bundled me up and we were on our way. Soon after we arrived at the hospital, the contractions started. The very first pain was horrific. I had been told by my doctor that the pain would be gradual. As the contractions became more frequent, the pain increased and it seemed more than I could bear. Nonetheless, I was in hard labor for approximately eight to ten hours. I don't remember exactly. It was painful as well as stressful going through labor with Mama. I think she was angry with Tim. I will rephrase that, I *know* she was angry with Tim. She kept shaking her head and biting her bottom lip. She hated seeing me go through all of that pain. I hated experiencing it with her because I could see the hurt in her eyes for me. I thought about her pain while I was in pain. I look back on that time now, and I can laugh. The baby's daddy should be present in the labor room so you can slap him a time or two if necessary. I know Tim would have been there with me, if we had told him to come. I went through the most excruciating pain and sweating I had ever experienced in my life. I thought it would never end. I felt like my body was being torn to pieces and ripped apart.

Wow, *finally*! It's a beautiful girl! We had a beautiful *healthy* baby girl. I was exhausted physically and mentally. My eyes even hurt. She had a full head of black hair and big beautiful eyes. I was instantly smitten and in love with my baby. Yes, I wanted to keep her. It was amazing to me that something or someone so beautiful could have been formed and lived on the inside of me for nine months. Thank You Jesus that I didn't kill my baby! My God is an *awesome God!* After she was born, I did let Margie name her Margo Denise Smith. I liked that name also. I was so enamored when I saw my baby, but then the nurse told me it would be best if I didn't see her anymore. "Why," I exclaimed. The nurse said it would make it more difficult for me to leave her there in the hospital.

I cried after the nurse took her away. I kept thinking, "I'm not going to be able to do this." After the nurse took her to the nursery, another nurse came in and gave me a shot to stop my breast from filling up with milk. Wouldn't you know it though, the shot didn't work. I had so much milk my breast were as hard as bricks engorged with milk. I had pain at my top and my bottom. I could not believe it. No one had told me anything about this milk filling my breast and hurting. This was just something else for me to cry about.

Late that night, I snuck down a dimly lit hallway to the nursery and saw Margo again. Amazingly no one saw me. For some reason the curtains were open at the big window in the nursery. I believe that God was giving me one last chance to see Margo and to pray over her. "Father God protect my baby. Let her be brought up in the nurture and admonition of You. God please don't allow her to hate me because; I am not giving her away, I am leaving her with You, Amen." She was still the most beautiful baby I had ever seen. She had the prettiest dark eyes. She was perfect.

I said again to myself, "I don't know if I can do this. God please help me. This is too hard, too painful. I don't know if I can do this." I was crying that out from the depths of my soul. "I don't know if I can do this." I slowly returned to my room. Of course I cried myself to sleep. I never saw my baby girl again while she was an infant.

CHAPTER 14

The After Shock!

I WAS HOSPITALIZED FOR FOUR days. The doctor was still trying to dry up the milk in my breast and I was still in some pain. The day I was discharged from the hospital, Mama, Alvin and Margie came for me. When we left the hospital we went straight to an attorney's office to sign the adoption papers. That was no surprise. Alvin had told me that was where we were going. I don't remember much about that meeting besides the fact that the attorney asked me to sign a stack of papers. I did willingly sign those papers. Then I remember the attorney looked directly in my eyes and said, "Jacqueline Iona Smith, you understand now that you are no longer the legal mother of Margo Denise Smith. You are now the legal aunt of Margo Denise Smith."

That was the first time it really registered in my mind that adoption was for real and permanent. Hearing him say I was no longer the *legal mother* of my baby that I had carried and nurtured for nine months was startling. The baby I had just spent ten hours in pain delivering. Signing away my legal right to be her legal mother would not sink in my brain. *Legal?* He said I am not her mother. I was in shock and had no recourse. I never thought about anything legal. Legal?

He repeated, "Do you understand?"

After a long pause and several swallows, I said in a whisper with tears in my eyes, a quiver in my voice and deep pain in my heart, "Yes." I was totally devastated, in fact traumatized again.

I guess I never thought through or expected this kind of heartache. How could I be prepared for this? My brother and I never really talked about this part. *Legal?* I barely knew what legal meant. It has to do with the law. You have to remember I was still in actuality a freckled faced kid. Emotionally this was too much for me to take in. When we left the law office I told Mama, "We have to leave here before I change my mind. We have to go to West Virginia." Mama agreed that we should leave right away. We did.

I had so many mixed emotions. I was thankful that my baby was healthy. She had ten fingers, ten toes and no physical or mental defects. I knew that Alvin and Margie would take really good care of her. She would have the best doctors, parents and all she would ever need. More importantly, I was leaving her with God. He was my assurance. Nevertheless, despite all of this assurance, I wanted my baby. I wanted to hold her and to give her all the love I had built up in my heart for her during the nine months I carried her. I had protected her from all the railing accusations, whispers, and gossip behind my back from people who were disappointed in me for getting pregnant. I wanted to love her and have her look in my eyes and recognize me as being the voice she had heard from conception. I wanted to let her know today that *I am her legal mother.* I wanted to tell her that

I wanted her and loved her with all of my heart. I wanted to let her know that it was not my decision not to keep her with me.

I wanted to tell her that I would always be there for her no matter what. To tell her I had no physical or financial way to take care of her right then, and that I was not giving her away, but I was leaving her with my Father God. He promised me He would take good care of her. So I left her with God.

CHAPTER 15

More Difficult Days Ahead

ON THE BUS RIDE back to West Virginia, I sobbed as my whole body shook. I continued to cry silently. Mama really didn't know what to do or say to me. She would just give me napkins to wipe my face and tell me, "It'll be all right." I think she was surprised I went through with the whole adoption process. I think she knew that several times during those proceedings, I wanted to stand up and scream at the top of my voice, *stop no, I can't do this!* I know it was the love of God for Margo, Alvin and Margie that restrained me. I didn't realize that I was suffering from post-partum depression. This is a condition some mothers experience as a delayed mental and emotional depression or sadness after giving birth. Hormones fluctuate as they attempt to get back to normal. I am not an expert on the physiology of this condition. I just know how I was affected. I was also grieving the loss of my baby. It took me some months to get my head on straight. I often felt sick to my stomach.

Mama was such a trooper. She suffered through this whole transition with me, and I know she hurt just as much as I did. She really didn't know how to comfort me. She was just there.

Yes, I love her forever. We were not a huggy-kissy type family. We did embrace when we had been apart for a while, and we hugged when we left each other, but other than that we didn't touch a whole lot. I understood Mama wanted to hold me in her arms and make the pain go away, but she didn't know how.

The bus ride home was a very long one. Mama had taken this same long ride to Michigan to get to me five days earlier. It was over four hundred miles and all the way I wondered what my daddy would say to me. How would I be received? After all, as he'd said, *I was not bringing a baby in that house.*

When we arrived in Huntington, we caught a taxi to the house from the bus station, and I found out what my daddy would say to me. *Nothing*. I said, "Hi Daddy," and he just grunted. As days went on, Daddy said nothing to me at all. We sat in the same room together watching something on television in silence. At other times when I entered the room, he left.

The pain and guilt of all of how deeply I had disappointed him was almost unbearable. To attempt to soften the emotional toll this was taking on me, Mama acted just the opposite. She talked to me more than usual, always asking me questions. She would say, "How are you feeling today? Are you healing up all right down there? Have you talked to Ann today?"

Her questions were saying to me, "Please stop being depressed." I love my mother because even though she is in heaven today, her caring presence and tender attentiveness to me all of my life still warms my heart.

My beautiful Mama didn't know what to do or how really to help me move forward. She did whatever she could to buffer the rejection she witnessed me receiving from my daddy.

The grieving was horrendous, yet I knew I must continue to live, continue to pray and continue to move ahead. I cried a lot for no apparent reason. It was difficult for me to concentrate. I didn't know anything about post-partum depression in those days. But, as I have become more knowledgeable about my body and female hormones, I am convinced that I suffered with the deep depression for many months after Margo's birth. Also, as I have thought about how I suffered those many months; I was going through the stages and severe waves of grief. *I didn't have my baby!* Prayer helped me more than words of encouragement or sympathetic actions. I would pour my heart out to God constantly. Mama kept praying for me also. God continued to assure me everything would be fine if I would continue to trust Him, so I did. I also had to deal with the people who knew that I was pregnant when I left home but came back without a baby. They had curiosity in their eyes, and on their faces yet they were cordial to me. I just continued to live my life with my head up and a smile on my face; thanking God every day that I was alive, and so was my baby.

As God would have it, President Lyndon Johnson had initiated some war on poverty programs for low-income persons in 1964. That would be me. I was a *no* income person and thankfully there was one of those programs in Huntington. My pastor shared the information with me.

I enrolled in a class that taught typing and shorthand. The class was held five days a week which was wonderful for me. The program gave participants a stipend of something like forty dollars every two weeks. I might not have those figures exactly right but I am close. I looked at that program as being Jehovah

Jireh, my provider God providing something for me. Whatever it was that I received every two weeks, I gave Mama half and was so thankful I could give her anything.

When I got back to Huntington I learned that Tim had left town and moved away, which I know was God also. I still cared about him, but I would not allow my thoughts to dwell on him. I didn't know where he went and didn't ask.

My sister-in-law Margie sent me two little baby pictures of Margo when she was a few weeks old. I put those pictures on my desk while I did my work every day. Although I did cry daily, looking at her inspired me to continue to live. I knew that as she grew and knew that I was her mother, she just might want to come and live with me. I never wanted to confuse her. It was important to me that she knew that I loved her and never wanted to give her up. I also wanted to keep my word with my brother Alvin and Margie and not interfere causing any anxiety for them or Margo.

I completed my classes, learned to type and write shorthand. That was progress for me. I had a longing to leave home, go back to Denver, get a job and start a new life in Christ Jesus. I really liked Denver. By now, almost nine months had passed. God had done a great job of continuing to heal my broken heart and ailing body. Margo had not been an easy delivery. Also God was continually assuring me that Margo was well taken care of and was loved beyond what I could have ever imagined.

The endurance, patience and perseverance I had developed in the past year had made me fearless. I felt like I could tackle the world. I was ready to go. My faith in Jesus Christ was stronger than it had ever been. I had proof now that He loved me and would take care of me. I knew for sure that God was faithful and would never leave me or forsake me. I was confident that He would walk me through life. Proverbs 3:26 says For the Lord shall be your confidence, firm and strong and shall keep your foot from being caught in a trap or some hidden danger. I believed every word of that scripture then and I still do today. I was fearless and ready to live my life. After attempting suicide a year earlier, God was giving me another chance to live, and gratefully I took that chance.

CHAPTER 16

A New Life in View

I CALLED MY BROTHER JIMMY and *sister-in*-love Bonnie in Denver and asked if I could come back there and stay with them temporally until I could find a job and get an apartment. They said yes. I think they wanted me to come out of Huntington and not get stuck there where I might find myself in an unhealthy pattern of life. I was more than excited to go.

My relationship with my daddy had improved some, at least he was talking to me now. Yet, I think he wanted me out of Huntington also for my good. A few weeks later I was ready to go. The Chesapeake and Ohio train was leaving in the early morning hours of the next day. The night before I left, I went to my father shortly before his bedtime. I told him I was going to move to Denver, get a job and start a new life.

I asked Daddy if he could give me anything to help me on my way, I would appreciate it. Collectively, Mama and I had spent everything we had getting my clothes cleaned and buying necessities. My daddy pulled out a twenty dollar bill and told me to go to the store and buy him a Coke. I was so excited because if he gave me the change from that twenty dollars, that would have been plenty to help get me to Denver. Some of my friends were having a party that night at the American Legion on Tenth Avenue. I called it my going away party even though it wasn't. I had left the party which was still in progress. I had on high heel pointed toe shoes. I ran all the way, one block to the store, rushing to get back to daddy with that Coke a Cola. I gave him his change. He gave me back two dollars. Yes, I said two dollars.

I was so hurt. I looked at Mama, then I looked at him and I said, "Thank you Daddy. I appreciate it very much."

I uttered those words but that crushed me and Mama again. I took a big swallow and a deep breath went back to my friends' party, and *my pretend* going away party and I danced. I'm reminded of the song that is entitled, *"I Hope You Dance."* Here is one of the verses:

> *I hope you never fear those mountains in the distance, never settle for the path of least resistance; living might mean taking chances but they're worth taking, loving might be a mistake but it's worth making. Don't let some hell- bent act leave you bitter; when you come close to selling out reconsider. Give the heavens above more than just a passing glance, and when you get the choice to sit it out or dance, I hope you dance.*

That is precisely what I did. I made the choice to dance. I hold nothing against my daddy. I love my daddy with all of my heart. Often people do and say things to you because things have been done and said *to* them. My daddy let me know later on in life that he loved me very much and was real proud of me. Sadly, he didn't know how to say it or show me at the time.

As I grew older and wiser I began to understand that hurting people hurt people. I don't blame him for it. Some of the things my daddy did or didn't do to and for me have helped me learn to practice the power of true forgiveness. God blessed our relationship greatly years later. Moreover, I learned that even though he was a deacon in the church, he wasn't saved. He had never asked Jesus to come into his heart.

In 1975 while my father was in the hospital, I told him he didn't have to live his life being angry anymore.

> Because if you acknowledge and confess with your mouth that Jesus is Lord [recognizing His power, authority, and majesty as God], and believe in your heart that God raised Him from the dead, you will be saved. For with the heart a person believes [in Christ as Savior] resulting in his justification [that is, being made righteous—being freed of the guilt of sin and made acceptable to God]; and with the mouth he acknowledges and confesses [his faith openly], resulting in and confirming [his] salvation. (Romans 10:9-10 AMP)

Daddy said, "I know that." So, I Praise the Lord that God gave me the humbling honor and privilege to pray with my daddy and lead him to the Lord. Two weeks later he went to heaven. I tell you love never fails. I have received many honors and rewards in my lifetime, yet none compare with leading my father to God, our Father.

CHAPTER 17

It Won't Be as Long as It's Been Bein'

My move to Denver coincided with the flooding of the Big Thompson River in June of 1965. At that time the Big Thompson River in Colorado had overflowed its banks. I had only two dollars in my pocket, the change from the Coke-a-Cola, which my father had given to me for this trip. My lack of funds became a significant factor. I bought a big bag of potato chips, some candy and had only change left when I boarded the train. That meager amount had to last me for the two day trip from Huntington, to Denver. As it turned out the trip lasted four days. The tracks were flooded all along the way, especially in Nebraska. The train actually sat on the tracks somewhere in the state of Nebraska for twenty- four hours. With the chips and candy eaten, my need for food increased rapidly.

There were three or four African American porters and cooks on that Chesapeake & Ohio Railroad Train. These men who served others for a living were adept at judging folks and knowing what they were about. They had no trouble sizing me up. Those gentlemen knew I was penniless. One of them looked to perhaps be someone's very non-threatening gentle grandfather. He kept coming through the train car speaking to me. He asked where I was going, I told him Denver. He said, "I haven't seen you in the dining car." I said, "No I'm not hungry." I was really afraid to talk to him. After all he was a stranger. I had no idea what his intentions were. This was my first time riding a train alone, and with me going on my own for the first time, Mama had warned me to be cautious of men who might want to take advantage of me. She always used to say, "Be careful and don't take no wooden nickels." To me that meant, don't be deceived. Don't let anyone con me or talk me into a place or position where I could be harmed or taken advantage of.

Another kind looking man was the cook. He kept coming back talking to me. He too seemed to be a nice person. He was a middle-aged African American gentleman with an amiable face, who appeared to be genuinely concerned about me. I perceived he probably had a daughter just by the tender and concerned way he approached me. His eyes seemed sincere and the tone of his voice was like that of a caring father.

He asked, "Why don't you come to the dining car and have a nice dinner on me? It won't cost you a dime."

"Oh no," I replied, "I'm not really hungry." I sat there for a long while and reasoned in my mind; he can't rape me on this train with all of these people here. When I get off the train, I know my brother will be waiting for me, and I will just run to him and be safe. Maybe I will go back there and see if I can eat something for free. After all I hadn't eaten a full meal in two days. I prayed and asked God to protect me. I took a chance and went to the dining car, and those warm-hearted gentlemen said,

"Well look who's here. Sit down right there and let us buy you dinner." I know God had positioned those men there like the ravens who fed Elisha in the Bible. (1 Kings 17:4, 6) They served me the biggest steak, baked potato and salad I had ever had in my life. As Mama would've said about my hunger, "You were so hungry, you won't know if it was good or not until tomorrow."

The train's cooks and waiters took real good care of me. Not one of them ever made any improper advances toward me. Instead they made jokes and tried to make me feel comfortable as they served me. So, I relaxed and engaged them in conversation. They asked about my family, and I told them that I was the eighth of nine children, and that I was going to Denver to start my new life. One of them asked, "Are you going to stay with relatives?"

"Yes, I replied, I was going to live with my older brother and sister-in-law until I could find a job." They thought that was a good plan for me to be with my brother in the big city of Denver. They all wished me well as I finished my dinner and returned to my seat. Their wisdom and experience told them the obvious. I was just a scared little girl coming out of West Virginia without enough money to get to where I was going. Moreover, as a result of their wisdom, they teamed up to help me get to Denver safely.

After I ate I thanked them several times. I wished I had gone to the dining car sooner. I even had leftovers to take back to my seat. I was happy, full and sleepy now, but we still had another day to go before we arrived in Denver. Now as Mama used to say, "It won't be as long as it's been bein'." That meant I had a shorter time before I got to my destination now than I did when

I started. Those timely words that Mama had spoken to me in her own vernacular over the years, became more comforting and meaningful then and as I have continued on my life's journey.

CHAPTER 18

Love on the Horizon

One of the definitions of hope is favorable and confident expectations. Strong hope had risen in my head and heart for my move to Denver at the age of nineteen. I arrived in Denver safely, and oh was I glad to get there. I felt like the train had carried me to the promised land, but I was too tired to dance.

My brother Jimmy met me at Union Station in lower downtown Denver. He was upset because the train was delayed three days. No one had contacted him to tell him where the train was. In the sixties, no one had cell phones, so naturally without any news, he had been worried about me. We embraced while I quickly explained to him that the flood had delayed the train. Those porters and cooks who fed me well and watched over me during my trip, came to the car where I exited the train. I waved at them. I told Jimmy how they had fed me. They all smiled and waved back at me as I yelled, "Thank you again for everything."

I experienced great peace after getting settled in my brother's home. I rested up for a week then I went to look for a job. I received two offers, one from the Mountain Bell Telephone Company and one from the Central Bank and Trust downtown.

I took the offer from the Central Bank and Trust mainly because my brother Jimmy ran the computer department there. I was ecstatic. This was the first real job I'd ever had in my life.

I called Mama and told her about my job working as a verification clerk in the credit department. When I told her how much money I would be making she was so happy for me.

She exclaimed, "Great, Just keep doing good and don't take no wooden nickels.

I laughed. I could feel how relieved she was that I was safe, doing well and happy. I lived with my brother Jimmy and Bonnie for 3 months.

Life was good. By the grace of God, I was quite pleased with the progress I had made over the past few months. I endeavored to be as independent of my brother as possible, and he wanted me to be.

I had joined Zion Baptist church and met a few friends. Kathy Peden was one of those friends. Kathy was kind and a Christian much like the friends I was used to in Huntington. Also my brother introduced me to Jenifer. Jenifer introduced me to one of her friends Sherri Gossett who called me one day and asked if I wanted to go swimming. I said,

"Yes absolutely." I enjoyed swimming and swam a lot growing up. I hadn't been swimming for a long time so I was excited to go with her. I didn't realize Sherri was being escorted by three of her male friends. One of them got out of the car and was peering into my brother's picture window. She introduced the guys to me. There was Charles, Buba Do, and this cute guy who was driving the car, and peeping in the window was Ronnie Calloway. I had already heard his name from a few ladies. To say Ronnie had a reputation as a ladies' man would definitely be an understatement. Believe me, I didn't know what being a ladies' man actually meant at that time. I was so green coming from West Virginia. I had also never heard the words prostitute or marijuana. Even though I had given birth to my baby Margo, I truly had been sheltered from worldly people and environments. I had no street smarts at that time to speak of. I was quite naïve. I was trusting God to lead me, enjoying my job and my new-found life in Denver.

Sherri and I went swimming that day at Skyland Pool, but the guys didn't come inside the pool. They just dropped us off at the gate. I swam for about thirty minutes. When I came out of the water I was sunbathing near the pool. To my surprise, someone was throwing pebbles at me as I lay on my stomach. Guess who? Mr. *cute* Ronnie Calloway. He wanted to talk so I went to the fence. He wanted to know what I was going to do after we left the pool. I was nice to him but I didn't have much to say. I was not interested in getting into another relationship with a dude especially another cute dude. As Ronnie drove Sherri and me home, he kept smiling at me through the rearview mirror. I acted like I didn't notice. I thanked him for the ride and I didn't hear from him again.

Of Course

A week or so later, Jimmy, Bonnie and I went to a dance to see the Impressions singing group at the Baha ballroom in downtown Denver. I had never been to a grown people's dance, which featured a famous nationally known singing group. I was so excited. I was enjoying the music and singing along with the Impressions. It was fun seeing Jimmy and Bonnie and all the other people dancing. I was having a great time. As I gazed across the room I spotted Mr. Ronnie Calloway just coming in the door alone. I walked slowly across the dance floor to say hello. I asked, "Hi, Ronnie, do you remember me?" he turned, smiled and said,

"Of course I remember you. How could I ever forget you with your pretty self?"

With his next breath he asked, "May I have this dance?" Of course it was a slow dance. He told me how good I smelled. He was such a smooth operator I had to be cautious. He asked if I was with anyone. I told him I was there with my Jimmy and Bonnie.

He said, "Oh I know them, let me go and say hello to them." My brother knew of him through some mutual friends of theirs. After he spoke to Bonnie and Jimmy, we danced again. I thought He was a decent dancer. I knew I was a great dancer. After all, that is what I spent half of my time doing growing up in West Virginia. All of my friends knew all the latest dance steps. We learned to dance at an early age and perfected our steps as we grew up. During that dance Ronnie asked me to hang out with him for the rest of the evening. He wanted to introduce me to some of his friends. I agreed and the night turned into a most memorable occasion. It seemed that he knew almost everyone in that ballroom. We went from table to table meeting his friends. Ronnie wanted them *all* to meet me. We laughed and talked and sang while on and off the dance floor. I told him he could not sing so let the Impressions handle the music. He had a great sense of humor, and that was admirable. That Impressions' dance was the most fun I had enjoyed in years. After the dance was over, Ronnie asked Jimmy if he could drive me home. Jimmy said,

"Yes, but drive her *straight* home."

"Of course," Ronnie replied.

Ronnie was very respectful to me. He did take me straight home. We said goodnight, I got inside the screen door and closed it. He opened the door quickly and kissed me on the lips gently and quickly; he closed the screen again and said,

"That should make the evening more exciting." Then he turned and walked away. I closed and locked the door behind me and thought to myself as I smiled, *I like that boy.*

After that night Ronnie started calling me every day. I did think he was cute. As time passed we got to know one another. He would take me to McDonald's for a cheeseburger and fries. We would go to Furrs' cafeteria for dinner. We talked about music, sports, and our ambitions. He loved golf, I liked football. We talked about what foods we liked. I found him to be very interesting. We laughed a lot and I liked that. Ronnie treated me like a queen. He opened every door for me and didn't use foul language at all.

One Saturday night Ronnie took me to another dance at the Baha Club in downtown Denver. While slow dancing Ronnie was holding me much too close. As we might say in West Virginia, I knew that he had taken a real shine to me. I asked him if we could go outside and talk. He was very anxious to do that. He had never been aggressive toward me in a sexual manner. But I could feel him getting mighty close to me. We went to his car which was right outside in the parking lot. He had a nice polished green 1951 Chevy.

He opened my door and we got in. I looked into his eyes and I told him, "You don't really know who I am or anything about me, but I want you to know who you were holding so tight tonight."

"On October 2, 1964 I had a beautiful baby girl, a real pretty little girl. My daddy would not let me bring her home with me to raise her, so my brother in Lansing, Michigan adopted her for now. Right now, I don't have her with me however, if she ever wants to come and live with me she can. No matter where I am, what I'm doing or who I'm with, she will be able to come live with me. Frankly speaking, I desperately want her to be with me."

Ronnie looked back into my eyes with all sincerity and said, "You know I love you. You didn't have to tell me all of that right now. I see you are honest, up front, and you know what you want. I appreciate that." Then we went back inside the Baha and continued *to dance.*

About a week or so later Ronnie brought me some flowers. He looked at me and said, "I have never met anyone I felt like I want to live the rest of my life with, so will you marry me?" Contrary to what I thought or had been told, he didn't seem like such a ladies' man to me if he wanted to get married so fast. I thought he was kidding.

I liked to sit and listen to older people talk to me. I recognized at an early age that some of them had wisdom. Mrs. Cora Washington who was probably sixty when I was seven, lived two doors from our family home. I would go to her house and sit on the front porch with her often. I was about seven or eight when she told me, "Jackie, if you pray and ask God to send you the husband *He* wants you to be with, He will." I told Mama what Mrs. Washington said and we prayed from that time on for my husband.

When Ronnie asked me to marry him I prayed, "God, is this my husband?" The answer was yes, but He didn't tell me to marry him right then. I believe He wanted me to have a more intimate relationship with Jesus Christ and He wanted Ronnie to get saved. None of that happened right away. Nonetheless, I said yes to Ronnie and his proposal.

When I told my brother about Ronnie's proposal, Jimmy had a fit. He had known Ronnie before I met him. He knew him to be a playboy, and he was absolutely right. I was going to have to learn that for myself. I called Mama and told her I had met a guy who was very nice to me and who was showing me all the respect that I deserved. I told her that he doesn't use profanity, he opens every door, and he holds every chair out for me, shows and tells me he loves me every day. And best of all, when he spends his money on me, he doesn't ask for anything in return.

Mama responded, "I think you have been through enough to know what you want. If you like him, you do what you think is best."

That was all I needed to hear. Ronnie and I married on August 27, 1965 at Zion Baptist Church. We had just a small wedding with mostly family and friends but it was beautiful. Reverend Liggins married us. The best part of the day was that Mama flew in for our wedding. The first time Mama met Ronnie she liked him. We were all very happy. One of Ronnie's friends gave us a small reception at her house. I was nineteen now and Ronnie was twenty-one. I hardly knew anybody at our wedding. They were mostly Ronnie's friends and family.

I did remarkably well going on with my life after our wedding. God does all things well, even healing hearts. I definitely had trusted Him to heal me from all I had experienced. It was a joyful process. In all of my moving forward in life, having to overcome wounds and grief, God has proven to me that He is faithful. He is truly *more* than enough in every situation.

Approximately one year after we were married, Ronnie and I both wanted desperately to have a baby. We tried and tried but I couldn't get pregnant. I thought, "Oh no this can't be happening. My brother has adopted my daughter and now I can't have other children?"

I went to an Ob/Gyn doctor who told us it was impossible for me to get pregnant because my tubes were blocked. There was some type of infection, and he said he needed to schedule a hysterectomy right away. I told him he could schedule whatever he wanted, but in one month I would be pregnant. He reluctantly followed my instructions to let me wait and scheduled the surgery for over one month later. Well, one month from that day I went back to see him and I was pregnant. The doctor was shocked.

Ronnie and I had two daughters Rhonda Lynn and Chaunci Yolonda two years apart. They were such a joy to us as I yielded to God's call to be their mother. Motherhood truly is a calling. God entrusts us to deliver those babies into the earth realm because He has a purpose and assignment for them. He gives us the opportunity and privilege to help them fulfill their assignments in life. Our job is to nurture, observe, discipline, pray and discover their God given bent or tendencies and talents. Then you can help them develop in those areas. My relationship with my Daddy had improved drastically. I would take Rhonda and Chaunci to Huntington and spend a month with my parents every year. I wanted them to know and be influenced by them both. My Daddy loved them dearly and took them for a walk every day. He also gave them money and bought them shoes for Easter every year. God does Miracles.

By allowing me to give birth to three healthy girls, I realized God stopped me from killing my babies. Satan tempted me to kill myself when I was a pregnant teenager. He was after *all* of my babies. Not just Margo but all of my babies and their babies too. That included all of my five grandchildren who are now grown people with lives and assignments of their own. I pray for them every day that they will fulfill God's purposes for their lives. I also know we all make our own choices in life. However, I didn't deny them the opportunity to make those choices. They are living their lives because I didn't kill myself and my babies at age seventeen. Don't kill your babies.

Those babies I had not conceived yet when I was a confused teenager, could have been denied their right to life. That was a demonic decision to kill myself. Don't kill your babies.

> **But Jesus said, Suffer little children, and forbid them not, to come unto me: for of such is the kingdom of heaven. (Matthew 19:14)**

God loves babies and children. He says we are made in His image and His likeness.

One translation of the Bible says, "Leave the children alone!" I believe He is speaking about those children who are still in the womb also. Allow them to come unto to Him. Don't kill them before they are born, like I almost did.

Life is so sacred to our God. He is the one who creates and brings forth life. What did Jesus say?

> The thief comes only in order to steal and kill and destroy. I came that they may have *and* enjoy life, and have it in abundance [to the full, till it overflows]. (John 10:10 AMP)

The thief is Satan. To terminate a baby's life in the womb is eliminating our future doctors, preachers, congress persons, presidents, mothers and fathers. We desperately need boy babies to become Godly fathers to so many children who don't or won't have healthy role models. We don't know who God has designed any of these unborn children to be.

Ronnie and I have a 6'6" handsome grandson Azlan who is now twenty eight years old. This boy calls us almost every day to check up on us to make sure we're okay. Before Azlan hangs up the phone, he tells me and Ronnie he loves us. No he is not perfect but, who he has become brings much joy to us and his mother Rhonda. He told me, "Gee Gee, and Dee Dee are my grandma names, I am so glad you didn't kill me." I told him that I am glad I didn't kill him and our other four grandchildren Jacqui, Elyse, Joshua, and Julia whom we love dearly. They are able to be who God has called them to be because I didn't kill my babies. God always has a future and hope for you and those children you might bear. You just have to trust the process called life. Don't kill your babies and don't kill yourself. There are so many organizations today that will help you keep and raise your baby. There is always hope and help you just have to ask for help and remember God loves you and your baby.

CHAPTER 19

Trust God All the Way

EVEN THOUGH I KNEW Margo was safe, loved and well cared for, over the next several years, Satan still tried to work on my mind. He brought negative thoughts to me saying, "You abandoned your first born child. She will have abandonment issues the rest of her life. What kind of mother could just give her baby away and go on with a carefree life? She thinks you didn't want her. Your family thinks you're crazy anyway, talking about God told you to do this." More of those thoughts crept into my head and occasionally caused me to cry myself to sleep at night.

Ronnie was a comfort to me during those times. Sometimes he held me in the night, comforting me saying, "You know you did the right thing because you obeyed God." He then pulled me tight to him and whispered in my ear, "Do you want to make another baby right now? I'll be glad to help you do that." His wide grin and those words always made me laugh. I love that guy. Then God, my Father, would remind me, "You didn't give Margo away; you left her with Me." Those words always gave me peace, and I continued to do what He had asked me to do, "Trust Me." I *had* to trust Him. I had to *trust Him all the way*. I couldn't doubt all of those wonderful things He did for me. I can't forget how faithful He had been. I always have to go back to the word of God: which says,

> **Casting down imaginations, and every high thing that exalteth itself against the knowledge of God, and bringing into captivity every thought to the obedience of Christ. (2 Corinthians 10:5)**

I know who God is in my life and I know He is faithful. I don't ever want to give Satan any credit for anything. I just want you to know that he is defeated and Jesus is Lord to the glory of God the Father.

My daughter Margo grew up to be one of the finest persons I know. God, my brother Alvin, Margie, and her Aunt Alma did an outstanding job of raising her. To be honest, our relationship was a bit strained during her teenage and young adult years. She was experiencing some challenges and I was as well. But Margo and I stayed in touch with each other, but not as consistently as I would have liked. Ronnie and I actually divorced staying apart for seven years after we had been married for twenty eight years. However, after those seven years we reconciled, remarried and became pastors and biblical marriage counselors. That story is told in my first book, *Love That Would Not Let Me Go*. That book details the miraculous events of how Ronnie and I divorced because of adultery, lies and drugs. Also the book describes how we forgave one another and came back together. It is a beautiful must read love story.

CHAPTER 20

God Does All Things Well

I HAVE NEVER BEEN A real social media fan because it can consume so much of my time. I had a Facebook and Twitter accounts because of the marriage ministry God called Ronnie and me to in 1998. The name of the ministry is the Repairer of the Breach Ministries, Inc. We were instructed to develop a website to supply married and single persons free help for their relationships. The name of that website was marriageinspiration.com which consisted of sound Biblical help.

I was on Facebook, trying to stay in touch with my grandchildren and my children. Margo and I communicated with each other from time to time on Facebook. I made it a point to see her when I went to Michigan, to visit other family members. Thus, we maintained a decent relationship. Even so, the relationship just felt a little distant to me. A mother wants to be close to her children.

Much to my surprise Margo came on Facebook and said to me, "Thank you for bringing me into this world." I was shocked. I responded,

"I wish I could have done so much more for you, Margo."

She replied, "You couldn't have done any more for me, you gave me life." I was overcome with emotion and joy. I logged off of Facebook and called her on the phone. I said, "It seems like for the first time you are really sincere about expressing your love for me."

"I've always loved and appreciated you, for your obedience to God for my good," she replied.

At this point I could hardly speak. My heart was flooded with joy and excitement.

I told her I never wanted her to think I didn't want to raise her. She responded that she never once thought that. She said, "I always knew I was loved by two mothers and two dads. I grew up thinking that was neat. I felt special."

Margo and I have become very close mother and daughter friends. We feel very comfortable with each other now. There is absolutely no guilt on my part for not having the opportunity to raise her. God is so good and can definitely be trusted. That is why He kept telling me to trust Him. After her initial Facebook posts and our telephone talks, Margo started calling me frequently. When she didn't call me, I called her. We have so much to talk about now. She has given us Ronnie and me a beautiful granddaughter, Elyse. We pray for her and all of our children every day. We are still catching up on the parts of both of our lives that we missed. It has been so exciting as well as fulfilling to get to know this intelligent, wise, beautiful woman that I left with God so many years ago. "He has done *all things well*." (Mark 7:37 KJV)

Holy Spirit had told me about two years before this encounter to write about reconciliation. I wrote for months thinking the reconciliation was again about Ronnie and me. I wrote all I knew about that reconciliation and then I was stuck. I couldn't think of one more thing to say. I stopped writing and put the manuscript away praying that God would give me what else He wanted me to say. Now that my reconciliation with Margo is complete, it dawned on me that my reconciliation with Margo was the relationship God wanted me to write about. This book is written and designed to give God all the glory honor and praise for all He has done in our lives.

Ronnie and I have learned in our years of counseling, that there are many women who find themselves in similar situations as mine, pregnant and unable to raise the baby for whatever reason. Be encouraged by my story to know this:

> **Trust in *and* rely confidently on the Lord with all your heart And do not rely on your own insight *or* understanding. In all your ways know *and* acknowledge *and* recognize Him, And He will make your paths straight *and* smooth [removing obstacles that block your way]. (Proverbs 3:5-6 AMP)**

CHAPTER 21

Another Turn of Events

I WANTED MARGO TO HELP me write this book. However, after reading the early manuscript she said to me, "Mom, I think this is your book to write. What you have to say is so important. So I give you permission to finish the book."

Of course, I was disappointed but she did want to add a little bit of our story in her own words.

> My Name is Margo. Wow, this is exciting for me to be able to share a tiny bit of my story with you. It is a miracle story indeed. My earliest recollection of being adopted was in kindergarten. Wisely, my parents explained to me the events surrounding my adoption when I was approximately four or five years old. I believe this was a

great move on their part to tell me "my birth story" while I was young enough to put together the names and faces. Needless to say, I was still too young to understand the gravity of the situation. Thankfully though, I just grew into the realization of our family dynamics.

My adoptive parents Al and Margie were really open about the situation early on. My adoptive mother and I flew to Denver to meet my biological mom and her family. I was perhaps four or five. I still have a picture from that trip. This was the first visual realization of having a unique family situation. I cannot remember feeling anything emotional about being adopted. I thought it was pretty cool to share in school, for show and tell, that I had two moms and two dads. At no time did I ever feel abandoned or even question why I was adopted. Whatever my dad told me, that is what it was.

I had a wonderful childhood. I grew up in a great neighborhood in a cul-de-sac full of kids all about my age. We actually all finished high school together. I was raised as an only child and was the apple of my father's eye. Life was good. My dad took his parenting responsibility very seriously. My adoptive mother did not work. She was always the stay-at-home parent throughout my childhood.

As a child I had no real intimate thoughts concerning my birth mother. I was totally entrenched in my childhood activities and sports. My adoptive mother made sure I called my birth mom on her birthday, which happened to be the same date as my Dad, her brother. I thought that was neat also. I would call my birth mom on Christmas and Mother's Day. Although I was shy, I was happy to call.

Whenever my biological mom came to town to visit my Grandmother and her siblings, I glad to see her. I never had a whole lot to say, as again, I was shy. I am so thankful to God that I am reconciled to my birth mom, my sisters and whom I call Uncle Ronnie. Another gigantic part of our miracle is that I am also reconciled with my biological father, Tim. He is now a clinical psychologist and is doing well. He and his family are a huge part of mine and my family's lives. He told me that he is a blessed man to have me in his life. They visit us often and I think he is a great man. I'm thankful to be his daughter. God has blessed us all. So, that is my story and I'm sticking to it.

CHAPTER 22

Who Is Margo Really?

Earlier on, I shared that God reveals a purpose to all of us who will listen to and follow His will. One of the revelations I have discovered about Margo is that she is a reconciler. A peacemaker. She has the uncanny ability to bring people together. She also does not hold grudges and encourages people to drop their rocks of revenge. She believes everyone should stop fighting, forgive and come together. I am so thankful for her and how she has enriched all of our lives in so many ways, by just being herself.

When Ronnie and I celebrated our fiftieth wedding anniversary, Margo and her kind husband Stan's gift to us was a trip to visit them in Tampa, Florida where they reside. When we arrived, she picked us up in this big orange truck. She was wheeling that big thing like it was a toy. I said, "This is a big orange truck."

"Yes it is," she replied.

She and Stan paid for our lodging in a Hilton hotel. Margo picked us up every morning, took us on tours of the area, fed us, and spoiled us for a week. They had even paid for Ronnie's green fees on the golf course for as many days he wanted to play. While Ronnie golfed, Margo and I spent time talking and shopping.

L-R Stan, Margo, Me, Ronnie, Rhonda's son Azlan, Chaunci, and Rhonda

One day we got a manicure and pedicure together. Then we picked Ronnie up from the golf course and went to some fancy restaurant overlooking the water on Tampa Bay. I think Margo knows almost every restaurant in Tampa and the outlying areas. The best part of the trip was that Margo and I talked for five days. I found out so many things I didn't know about her years growing up. I learned about the relationships she had with her uncles, aunts and cousins. How she views life and different aspects of it. I saw who she really is and I love her.

She has a personality a lot like mine. Margo loves big earrings and so do I. I have a huge collection. She really likes Stein Mart and used to shop there a lot and so did I. We even have some of the same blouses from Stein Mart. She is a no-nonsense person who loves to laugh and so am I. I think there is just something in a person's DNA when you conceive and give birth to a child that sticks. It doesn't matter if you raise that baby or not, a part of you is in them. That inherent quality comes from both the mother and the father.

Ronnie and I agreed that the gift that Margo and Stan gave to us for our 50th anniversary turned out to be the best vacation Ronnie and I have ever had. Ronnie was the one who said it first.

I guess what made the trip so fulfilling for me was that it solidified so many desires for me. I hadn't thought through how Margo had grown up and gone to school with her biological cousins. She had relationships with her biological uncles, my brothers, and aunts, my sisters. She knew Mama. Most of all I was so pleased to hear about the enduring and precious relationship she has with her biological father Tim. Again, Holy Spirit reiterated to me the faithfulness of God. He blessed us all in ways we could never have imagined. He had a plan from the very beginning for our lives.

Ronnie expressed to me how it blessed him to see Margo and me so genuinely engaged and happy. He saw there was no pretense or awkward moments in our conversations and time together. None at all. God gave us that trip to say, "Jackie I've got you. I always have had you, taken care of you and I always will." I praise Him for my life.

CHAPTER 23

The Conclusion of the Matter

I WROTE THIS BOOK TO encourage unwed mothers who might feel trapped, to know that *God* always has the *best* way for you. You may be in a situation where you don't know what you are going to do. God knows what you *should* do. He is waiting for you to ask Him and then obey Him.

> For I know the plans and thoughts that I have for you,' says the Lord, 'plans for peace and well-being and not for disaster, to give you a future and a hope. Then you will call on Me and you will come and pray to Me, and I will hear [your voice] and I will listen to you.
> (Jeremiah 29:11-12 AMP)

> Call to Me and I will answer you, and tell you [and even show you] great and mighty things, [things which have been confined and hidden], which you do not know and understand and cannot distinguish. (Jeremiah 33:3 AMP)

I remember vividly the night that I attempted suicide at age seventeen. I thought there was no way out of my situation, no hope and no future for me. However, God saw me and He sees you and He knows your heart. Pray to Him, call out to Him, He will reveal Himself to you.

I am begging all of you who read this book *not* to seek a permanent solution to a temporary challenge. If you feel ashamed or abandoned those feelings can change dramatically. They can quickly evolve into confidence and joy when you obtain the correct information. The Bible, God's word is the correct information.

In my story I had to be reminded that God loves me, thus I am reminding you that He loves you too. No matter where you find yourself or in what crazy situation *God loves you!* He sent His Son to die for you so that you and your baby can live a victorious life. There is so much help for you today. Help that God has provided.

But don't kill your babies and don't kill yourself. If you are having suicidal thoughts just know that it is the enemy talking to you. Remember John 10:10: Satan comes *only* to steal, *kill a*nd destroy. Jesus came that you might have *life* and have it more abundantly to the full until it over flows.

There are places that will take in you and your baby and care for you both. There is Lori's House for unwed mothers outside of Branson, Missouri, and the Denver Area Youth Services. You can search out other organizations that are there to help you. Make sure your babies know that you loved them enough to live. They also have a *right to life*. I recommend that you find a place that will also give you Jesus Christ and the word of God. He is your tangible help and *hope!*

To the parents of those daughters and sons who find themselves in similar situations as mine I say, don't kill your babies. I added sons because I know how heartbroken Tim was when he wasn't allowed to be a parent to his baby. Margo was and is his baby and a part of him who was taken from him temporarily. That taking left a horrendous void in his life. However, God always had a righteous plan. I have learned through my counseling experience over the last twenty five years that so many men and women are scared and wounded from some of the words and actions inflected upon them as children and teenagers by their parents. Parents, have mercy on your children. Don't kill them with harsh unforgiving words and attitudes. Imagine yourself in their place; think about how you would want to be treated and spoken to before you speak to them. Realize we've all sinned and come short in some area of our lives. All of us have. God forgave us and loved us while we were and are still in sin. Your children deserve the same compassion.

When I was pregnant, my father's words and actions could have caused me to become a bitter, angry and destructive person. It was only the Grace of God and my mother's wisdom that steered me in the right direction. If your children are willing to do the right thing after making a mistake, help them do the right thing. You do the right thing and *don't* kill the babies, yours or theirs.

Abortion is *not the right thing to do!* God says, "Thou shall not kill." So don't kill your babies. I have counseled both men and women who still experience guilt and regret for getting an abortion and killing their babies. Those stories are not highly publicized but there are many of them. Some of them still suffer emotionally as well as physically.

When I was pregnant, I knew that a life was growing on the inside of me. I knew it wasn't just a blob of tissue after just one month of pregnancy. Everything in me began to change. My sleep habits, my energy level, my nose began to widen, my eating habits, the frequency of urination, feet swelling. Everything changed. I knew life was on the inside of me. Then she began to flutter. I felt movement and kicking. When that baby is conceived that baby is alive. I don't care what anybody says. God our creator knew what He was doing. I am so thankful I didn't kill my future by committing suicide, and I didn't kill my babies. I pray that you won't either.

Now the *conclusion of the matter* is this. I love you and wanted you all to know that God is a miracle-working God. Because He has done all of this for me, He can and wants to do miracles in your life also. If you don't know Him and don't have an intimate relationship with Him, I beg you to do so for your own good. You can have a good life *here* and throughout eternity.

> **That if you confess with your mouth the Lord Jesus and believe in your heart that God has raised Him from the dead, you will be saved. For with the heart one believes unto righteousness, and with the mouth confession is made unto salvation.**
> **(Romans 10:9-10 NKJV)**

This simply states that, if you don't know Jesus Christ, ask Him to come into your heart out loud with your mouth. Ask Him to forgive you of your sins. Ask Him to fill you with His Spirit and you make Him the Lord of your life. Lord means ruler and director. Ask Him to be in control of your life and let Him do it.

Father God, I pray right now for everyone who reads this book. I pray that they will experience Your riches blessings, and will live the very best future that You have planned for them. Thank You Father that they have or will accept Jesus as their Lord and Savior. I call it done in Jesus' Name Amen. Father God I'm still in awe of You!

Post Script

Ronnie & Jackie Calloway

On December 7, 2020 my husband of 52 years, Ronnie Calloway, went home to be with the Lord. It could have been the worst day of my life, but on the contrary The Lord God Almighty graced us with time, precious time. Time to say to one another every single word that needed to be spoken before he left. I encourage you to look for my next book in which I pen our love story. One of the most compelling love stories of forgiveness and reconciliation you will ever read. The title of that book is *Till Death Do Us Part*. Look for it coming soon.

In 1997 my sweet Mama was diagnosed with Alzheimer's and went to be with the Lord June 15, 2001 at age 94. That is such a cruel disease. Some years earlier before she left, I asked God to give me just a window of time in which she would recognize me. He did that for me. For approximately ten minutes Mama came to herself. I said, "Mama do you know who I am?"

"Yes Jackie and you look so good." I quickly said to her, "Mama I love you so much. You have been the best mother anyone could have ever had. I thank God for you Mama." She smiled and replied, "I love you too." I thanked her for being a good wife to Daddy and raising all of us like she did. I also thanked her for introducing us to Jesus Christ. Soon there came a blank stare in her eyes and she left me mentally forever. Months later she went to heaven. I wrote this poem years ago about Mama.

MAMA

*Let's look back a moment children, to
the days of our childhood,*

when life seemed oh so simple, and living it was good.

*I awoke each morning to the sound
of Mama in the kitchen, trying*

to start us on our way our breakfast she was fixin'.

*To see her face when I came down
would start my day off right, she*

didn't have to smile you see her face gave off a light.

*It was then her task to see us off to
school that we might learn, to*

read and write to get a job, a better life to earn.

*But then upon returning from school
each day we'd meet, the aroma*

of some oxtail stew and hopefully pig feet.

*Mama didn't go to high school but to
work and had no choice but*

to help her deserted mother and be sensitive to her voice.

*But Mama knew the secret to living
life you see. Seek ye first the*

Kingdom of God she used to say to me.

*Be kind to all your brothers even
strangers you shall meet. Have*

hate in your heart for no one or yourself you will defeat.

*So by those very standards I've come
a long long way and thanking*

God for Mama each and every day.

*So if your mother is today alive and
by your side, show her the love*

within your heart, your affections you should not hide.

*For soon it may be oh too late for all
of us to say, "I love you Mama*

and hope you have a glorious Mother's Day."

Acknowledgments

I MUST FIRST AND FOREMOST acknowledge God the Father, God the Son, and God the Holy Spirit. He told me to write this book and directed my paths in doing so.

To Lauren Wilhoite-Willis, who for more than a year, edited the content and copy tirelessly. Thank you, one hundred times.

I acknowledge Pastor Felicia Smith who is one of my spiritual teachers. Thank you for your love and support.

To minister and friend of the family Carl Kennedy, you have prayed for me and our family since nineteen seventy-eight. We appreciate you more than words can express.

I also must acknowledge Marti and Reney DuBose. You both have loved and counseled us every time we've called. You've always *literally* had room for us over the years. Thank you and we love you back.

I acknowledge my sweet sister Miriam Riddle who is now 92 years young. I love you and acknowledge you just because you are still here trusting God and doing Great! Keep it movin' girl.

A loving thank you to Kimberly Stewart, my publisher. You have been more than patient with me and I appreciate that.

About the Author

JACKIE CALLOWAY IS THE author of *Love That Would Not Let Me Go*. She is an ordained minister, marriage counselor, reporter, television producer, broadcaster, and radio and television personality. She and her husband, Ronnie, are the founders of the Repairer of the Breach Ministries Inc. They have counseled and helped countless couples reconcile through Christ. They also host a radio broadcast bearing the same name. The Calloways reside in Denver, Colorado and have three children and five grandchildren.

Connect with Me

Jackie Calloway
P.O. Box 473368
Aurora, Colorado 80047
calloways1@hotmail.com
healingfromcrisis.com

www.ingramcontent.com/pod-product-compliance
Lightning Source LLC
Chambersburg PA
CBHW070506100426
42743CB00010B/1777